What Every Baby Knows

OTHER BOOKS BY T. BERRY BRAZELTON, M.D.

Infants and Mothers
Toddlers and Parents
On Becoming a Family
Doctor and Child
To Listen to a Child
Working and Caring
What Every Baby Knows

What Every Baby Knows

ॐ

T. BERRY BRAZELTON, M.D.

Ballantine Books • New York

Photo on page iv is by Hornick/Rivlin Studio
Photo of Mary Cotton on page 8 is used with the kind permission of Paul and Nancy Cotton.
All others drawn from videotapes of the cable television series *What Every Baby Knows,*
courtesy of Tomorrow Entertainment

Library of Congress Catalog Card Number: 87-91862

ISBN: 0-345-34455-3

This edition published by arrangement with Addison-Wesley Publishing Co., Inc.

Cover photograph by Hornick/Rivlin Studio. Reproduced by permission of Addison-Wesley
Publishing Co., Inc.

Manufactured in the United States of America

First Ballantine Books Edition: October 1988

10   9   8   7   6   5   4   3

To the families, the organizations, and the film crew who made this venture possible – we have learned so much together.

The publishers wish to thank Nancy Poland, R.N., for providing background material vital to the preparation of the manuscript, and for helping to coordinate continuing communication with the five families whose lives are portrayed in this book.

We are also grateful to Peggy Lamont and her colleagues at Tomorrow Entertainment, not only for initiating the wonderful cable series which inspired this book but also for generously making available the videotapes, transcripts, and other materials on which the book is based.

Finally, we wish to thank Joëlle Delbourgo, Vice-President and Editor-in-Chief of Ballantine Books' trade paperbacks, whose vision it was to bring *What Every Baby Knows* to the reading public.

Contents

Introduction

Over the course of my research into infant development at Children's Hospital in Boston I have become more and more aware of the many uses of videotape technology in science, education, and even psychotherapy. From filming the second-to-second expressions and reactions of newborns to teaching interviewing techniques to medical students, the potential of the medium continues to grow.

During the same period, as a writer and pediatrician, I've had several offers to host network television shows on childrearing. Unfortunately, the cost of making such shows, and their formats, meant that I would have to interview celebrities. I would have to sit there and ask these "talking heads" how they felt about being parents. I might, if I were lucky, uncover a certain amount of feeling in the process. I knew, however, that these shows would likely be shallow and rather useless, so I declined the offers. It was difficult to justify the time away from teaching and research at Harvard, training pediatricians, nurses, and psychologists at Children's Hospital, and a private practice. Nevertheless, the lure of the medium – to reach parents and those who make policy for children – remained strong.

In the early 1980s, Tomorrow Entertainment, a new cable TV company, conceived of a highly original parenting program. Tomorrow Entertainment had been founded by John Backe, former vice-president of CBS, and Peggy Lamont, a producer, who saw that cable offered a chance to do more in-depth shows, and also that the cost might be significantly lower. When they approached us (my wife always helps me make momentous career decisions), we were excited by the prospect of filming such vital issues as sibling rivalry and discipline with enough time left over to be able to look at what these issues really meant to both the child and the parents. As we talked, I saw again that the visual medium was very different from and potentially more powerful than books about childrearing. I knew that if a mother could see the difference between her child crying with colic and another child crying with acute pain, she'd never again think of "colic" as pain. I was thrilled with the challenge, the chance to dramatize these issues with real practicing parents.

Next, a crew had to be found whose goals were similar to ours. We needed a director, a filmmaker, and a cameraman who shared our interest in exploring childrearing with patience and seriousness. Peggy and John located a trio called New Screen Concepts, who had just won an Emmy for *The Body Human*. Lou Gorfain, Chuck Bangert, and Hank O'Karma were professionals, and they had children. As soon as I met them I began answering their questions, all about what it takes to be a good parent. Chuck's first question to me was, "How do I get my three-year-old to sleep through the night?" He'd hit on one of the most common problems for parents in the United States today. I knew we were a match! We were going to be able to work together. I promised him an answer, but in a half-hour show, not a one-line response.

Meanwhile, the all-important challenge of finding a sponsor for such innovative progamming was taken on by Beverly O'Malley and Erika Gruen of Dancer Fitzgerald Sample Advertising Agency. Thanks to their enthusiastic work, Procter & Gamble generously offered to sponsor the entire series.

Nancy Poland, a pediatric nurse practitioner and parent, works in the Child Development Unit at Children's Hospital with me. She enlisted the families who would be participating in the shows. She had had experience in teaching Lamaze classes, as well as putting together parent groups and answering their questions. Her intimate knowledge of parents and of their deepest concerns was critical to the success of our venture. We were asking young, struggling couples to discuss with us their most sensitive issues in front of a national audience. These couples knew they could trust Nancy, and they came to us secure in this trust. The kind of insight and honesty that we were able to elicit from them was in no small part due to the relationship Nancy had built with them.

The staff of the Child Development Unit played a vital role first in conceptualizing and then in fleshing out each issue. Our research there has for many years been centered around questions of attachment and communication between parents and infants. Normally stressed parents come with their small children to our clinic for help with a variety of childrearing problems. Our staff is multidisciplinary, from pediatricians and nurses to developmental psychologists. We have a "living laboratory" in which to explore these problems and in which to test the solutions.

Apart from the universal issues of growing up, we also explore the particular kinds of stress that impaired or difficult infants bring to a family. Conversely, we study the problems of poor or deeply troubled parents and how these affect their ability to parent. In all cases, we try to show parents that the answers to their problems can be found if they trust their own intuition and, more importantly, carefully watch and listen to their children. Our belief that "every baby knows" what is needed and will show a sensitive parent when things are off balance, is reflected in the title of the TV show and the book.

Our ongoing research was ideal as a foundation on which to construct a series of shows on childrearing. As we began to plan each show, we found that we had already set the goals and formulated the message we wanted to bring to parents. We knew the issues and their struggles. Our job was to communicate these insights to the families within the context of their daily lives. What constantly amazed me was how willing they were to share their deeper feelings on camera. The universality of their concerns became clear, and as we peeled away each layer we revealed a thoughtful honesty which became the hallmark of *What Every Baby Knows*. It was a thrilling experience for me to realize that I could now share the moments of insight and the relationships I had developed as part of my work in the privacy of my own office.

The proceeds we received from Procter & Gamble for our part in these shows have helped support child development fellowships at Children's Hospital. These fellowships bring pediatricians, psychologists, and nurse practitioners to Children's to study behaviorial issues in pediatrics. These people then carry this perspective into their teaching and clinical work throughout the United States.

Each chapter on each of the five families has four or five sections. The first is on the *family history*, gathered in preparation for the shows. It introduces the cast of characters. Following are two or three sections covering areas of concern. Each has three parts: the *office visit* uncovers the issues, such as crying, fears, or discipline, faced by the family. In it the dialogue reflects what happens every day in a pediatrician's office. These parts were drawn directly from videotapes of the office interviews with the families. Next, I discuss *the issues* themselves and try to reveal the universal developmental themes and some of the theory behind my advice. Finally, *questions* drawn from those asked by the studio audience, and most commonly asked by parents everywhere, round out the discussion.

The last section on each family is to me one of the most revealing parts of the book. Since we had gotten to know these families so well, I thought it would be exciting to follow them up and to learn how they had fared since, and how they had handled the problems they had discussed on the shows. Like so many childrearing issues, their concerns could not be resolved overnight, and called for a process of reorganization over a period of months or years. The ingenuity, energy, and continuing growth that all of these families have shown has taught me a great deal.

In these *follow-up visits* we discussed how the families had felt about appearing on the series. They told me that they only dared share their deepest concerns because they felt "safe" in doing so within the setting we had created, and because they also thought other families, suffering for the same kinds of reasons, might benefit. One couple mentioned that, before appearing on the show, they thought it would be safer to talk about their children than to reveal their own problems. Once they were interviewed on screen, however, they began to uncover their defenses, peeling back layer after layer of conflicts involving their own adult lives. Each family said that the experience was a real turning point for them. They had reorganized and faced the tensions they had uncovered with new insight. The growth I saw on screen continued. Their strength and ability to cope with their struggles was still evident two, even three, years later.

For readers who wish to understand more about our work at the Child Development Unit, Chapter VI, Learning to Be a Family, outlines briefly the family systems theory underlying this work. In this final chapter I make clear the link between the work that I did with the five families and the particular brand of behavioral pediatrics which we are developing in our fellowship program.

I hope that these glimpses into the lives of five real families are meaningful to the reader, as they have been to me, and to the viewers of our shows. People I meet on the street ask me, "What happened to the Cotton twins? Are they easier?" or "Has Linda gotten used to Andrew's leaving home?" or "How is that wonderful couple whose delivery we all shared?" Each viewer is touched personally by each family. They ask to be remembered to them.

And it is not just the adult viewer who becomes involved. Parents tell me their babies creep up to the television set to try to touch the other babies' faces. Older children ask searching questions of their parents after they've viewed a show. Parents use these viewing experiences to institute family discussions for settling their own trying issues. In addition, the shows are taped to train both college students in family development and home day-care providers.

Were it not for the generous and whole-hearted participation of five special families, *What Every Baby Knows* could not have come to pass. I enjoyed every moment working with Nancy and Paul Cotton, Linda Mazza, Susan and Tom Considine, Franci and Mark Sheehan-Weber, and Kathy and Joel Schwartz. To them, and to their wonderful children, I am deeply grateful.

The Cotton Family

❧

CHAPTER I

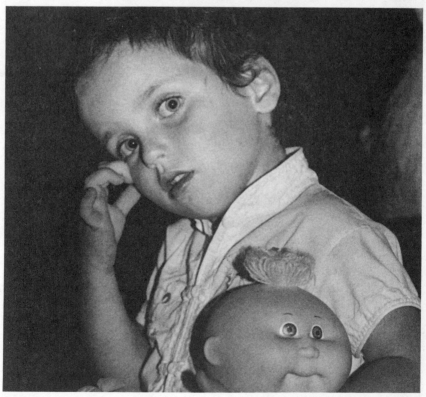

The Cotton Family

The Cotton Family

Family History

ॐ

Nancy Cotton, blond and vivacious, is in her late thirties. She had been a research assistant when she met Paul, then a medical student. When Paul finished his M.D., he became a psychiatrist. Now he is the medical director of a large psychiatric hospital. Nancy completed her Ph.D. in Developmental Psychology after they were married and went on to become a clinical psychologist. She is now director of an inpatient psychiatric unit at a local hospital. She calls her unit "family-centered care"; it was foremost among hospitals in metropolitan Boston in family participation in psychiatric children's care. Both Nancy and Paul are active, dedicated, upwardly mobile professionals – well-trained in their careers.

Before their three children were born, and since, the couple has been active socially and in the community. They work hard but they also play, both as a family and with friends. They enjoy traveling, skiing, summer vacations by the ocean, reading, and each other. They are happy, effective people who deeply appreciate their good fortune. Comfortable in their old-fashioned Boston house, they are surrounded with beautiful things, which they collect with enthusiasm.

Nancy says, "We've been fortunate. We have both worked, had money, and always enjoyed spending it. I have been able to afford and carefully choose live-in help so I could keep working after each baby or, in one case, babies! I knew it was important to me and to them. I got help because my work is critical to my sense of balance and well-being. My children and my clinical work enrich each other, and I'm a better person and mother for it."

After the birth of their first child, Anna, Paul became family oriented. He always did a significant amount of the housework and cooking, and now he took over some of the baby care. "Paul and I help each other in each area of our lives because we feel that this is part of being considerate of each other. We both like to cook and to keep the house straight. We often do things together. We share the babies. Paul gets as big a kick out of it as I do. He never wanted *his* children to be *my* children."

Anna was born seven and a half years after they married. Nancy says, "We wanted a baby but couldn't decide when to have one. Finally, we realized that we could not control everything, or time things perfectly. No one can predict the future. So we finally decided to go ahead and have a child as soon as possible. I grew up in Wellesley, in a middle-class family. Paul is also from a middle-class family, from Brookline. We were both privileged, lucky, and had lived well. By the time we had Anna, I was thirty-three, and our marriage and careers were established. We felt secure.

"Being an optimistic person, I guess I expected nirvana. Anna was difficult to deliver, and breast-feeding was a nightmare. Every time she nursed, it hurt. But I didn't want to miss the opportunity. I was so determined. I used a stopwatch to make sure Anna got enough milk, and I gave her a pacifier for recreation. When she was five weeks old, I went off to our summer house, on Martha's Vineyard. I wondered if it was the right decision because there was less in the way of family and friends for support. But we worked things out together that summer. She was energetic from the first, and I was constantly sleep-deprived, but we were, oh! so close. I found ways to make it easier for us. I found a babysitter to give me an afternoon break; I used the Swyngomatic so that I could eat a warm supper every once in a while, and I learned to give Anna pacifiers or bottles to soothe herself. She ended up using her orange juice bottle ("Ba Ba") until she was five years old. People objected, but I didn't care. I respect anyone's right and capacity to find comfort in their own way. Particularly for Anna, who was so competent, energetic, and outgoing. She needed to find times by herself to regroup – just like I do when I read. I love Anna's high intensity."

Paul interjected: "She was like a miracle to me. She was fabulous! miraculous! She even looked like me. I did as much for her as Nancy did, not out of guilt, but because I couldn't keep my hands off her. I took her with me everywhere when I was off work. At the Stop-n-Shop, all the ladies crowded around me, 'How do you do it? You're so good with her!'" As he talked of Anna, his cheeks flushed, his whole body actively described the dramatic and exciting times they had together. "I learned all about babies from her. I can bathe a kid faster than anyone in the world."

"My specialty in graduate school was infancy," continued Nancy. "I could tell you where their optimal focal point was, and I could follow their cognitive development, but I had no idea how to handle a baby. I was overstimulating Anna, and it was my hairdresser who taught me finally how to soothe, swaddle, and quiet her. It didn't make any difference what degree I had, I was an utter klutz!

"It was also hard, because I'd been at my job for a number of years. I found it difficult going back to being a rather inept beginner at a new thing like mothering. I'd become competent at my job and it was going smoothly. I remember being horrified one day when the doorbell rang. It was four o'clock in the afternoon. My hair was dirty. I was still in my bathrobe. I just couldn't believe I was answering the door like that, with the baby over one arm. I felt like someone out of a comedy routine. The first week I was home, I remember one night she was up all night long. Paul walked her in the Snugli. We read Dr. Spock about irritable babies. We couldn't get her back to sleep. The next morning I called you, Dr. Brazelton. I must have overslept and missed your calling hour. After answering my question, you politely reminded me about the calling hours. I felt like a fool. I wanted to defend myself. I felt like saying, 'Last week, you know, I ran a ward, I had a private practice, I was a perfectly competent person.' Now I couldn't even manage to telephone somebody at the right time."

"But that passed, too," said Paul. "Six weeks or so after you started, it was much better. It's one of the things that we learned, that hard times pass within a week, or month, or two months. Things change. We looked back at some old pictures we took of Anna when she was little and doing all sorts of things, a time that now seems almost from the remote past. We wonder why we took so many. But she seemed to us to be fantastic. All those comments, about how new parents are always saying that their kid is doing things that no other kid ever did before, were really true. Those feelings we had then really help now when the going gets tough. Certainly with the twins. It seemed so special, so unbelievable and so exciting, that we had two kids at the same time. I think a lot of

The Cotton Family

the hard work was more endurable because we felt so unusual. We felt special, in a way that was very helpful. We reminded ourselves: 'We have fraternal twins.'"

"I went back to work when Anna was three months," said Nancy. "I found full-time help. That way, I could enjoy her when I was home and get away when I needed to. I am a high-activity person, so I could understand a high-activity child like Anna. We could cycle together. I've never felt a bit of anxiety or ambivalence about her. I feel as if I've known her from the very first." Indeed, Anna is so much like both of her parents – dark and handsome like her father, pert and actively engaging like her mother – that she fell right in with their active, successful lives. They continued to work and play hard.

"Anna fit," said Nancy. "From the time she was born, we'd pick her up and just go. As you can see, going is pretty important in our family, and Anna thrived on it. We were not the only ones who enjoyed her; my own mother thought she was fabulous. She took care of her part-time after I went back to work. I had a chance to see my mother be loving and kind, a good mother to Anna. It was like reliving my own childhood – another kind of miracle. You see, I'd had a sister, Ginny, who had died. Anna gave my mother an opportunity to heal the pain of Ginny's death. This was true for me, too. We called her Anna Virginia after this sister. Ginny had a devastating mental illness. Her struggle for health, and the painfulness of her life, eventually helped me become a better therapist, and a more compassionate person. But there had been years of pain, anger, fear, and confusion for us all. Ginny's spirit, intelligence, and humor seemed to live again in Anna, but without the shadow of vulnerability.

"Then, while she was taking care of Anna, my mother had a stroke. She died within six months. Anna began to walk the week my mother died. I felt very alone. My father had died when I was a teenager. Now he and my sister and mother were all gone. Paul and Anna became even more important to me. Then, suddenly, I was pregnant again, and with twins. I felt as if I were given a gift of two little babies to replace the people I'd lost. I've always looked on them as a gift. When I heard I was going to have twins, my first thought was that I wanted it to be a boy and a girl. All at once, it occurred to me to call the girl Mary, after my mother, and the boy Billy, after my father. It seemed such a nice way to repair the loss.

"But it wasn't easy. First, they came prematurely at 35 weeks. I was lucky to have them in the hospital where I'd had Anna, where I worked. My obstetrician knew me and trusted me. We'd already done a baby together, so when Mary, who was first, was a breech, he let me deliver her without a caesarean section. Mary was such a little limp peanut that I guess I started worrying even then, although I blamed it on her prematurity. She wasn't responsive. Her Apgar scores [a brief test administered to newborn babies to judge their health and well-being] were very low – 4 and 6 [9 and 10 are best]. She had to go on a respirator, and her heart rate was always slow and irregular. She was in a special care nursery from the beginning.

"Billy was another matter. The first we saw of him was one arm waving – before he came out. He was ready to go. My wonderful doctor pushed his arm back in and delivered him gently without forceps or even tearing me. Although he weighed a pound less than Mary (4.4 pounds), he was so much stronger and more vigorous. He, too, had irregular breathing and heartbeat and had to be kept on monitors. But he was so lively from the start that I didn't worry as much.

"I had to stay in the hospital, my hospital, for nearly three weeks, taking care of them in the special care nursery, which was new, and had no curtains. It was like living in a fishbowl. It's a small hospital, and everyone knew me, so they all came by to see how I was taking it. I welcomed the support. The babies were both on monitors; everyone was afraid of SIDS (Sudden Infant Death Syndrome). Someone suggested that they go home with me on apnea monitors. After an initial 24-hour monitoring during their first period at home, we decided to take them off.

"The hospital did a great job for us, though. Billy sailed through it all. I nursed him; he gained weight, and I was ready to take him home after two weeks. Mary had to stay. She had poor neurological signs and a pitiful cry. She had a big hernia, was severely constipated, and her breathing and heart rate wouldn't settle down. I knew something was very wrong. She had me really scared. Sure enough, by the time she was three weeks old, the routine blood test they do for PKU and thyroid function showed that she had no thyroid working at all. We got her to Children's, where they began to treat her right away. We are pretty sure, as sure as one can be, that we got her in time to save her brain. She has responded so well to the thyroid medication that I'm sure she's OK."

Both Nancy and Paul have asked me this question on each visit, ever since we first picked up Mary's trouble in her early infancy. I have reassured them each time of my conviction that we caught her hypothyroidism so early there was no residual damage to her brain. We have had her tested repeatedly to confirm this, and every expert agrees with us. But parents can never get such a threat out of their minds completely. We all joke now about how it needs to be brought up so that I can reassure them on each visit. Yet it's no joking matter. Without the chance to share our concerns – theirs as parents and mine as their physician – we would be hiding an important question that could eat away at our image of Mary. Mary herself belies our concerns. She tests high on all cognitive tasks and is now catching up with her precocious, driving brother on motor tasks. At most, the period of hypothyroidism may have shaped her toward a quiet personality.

The twins were completely different. Billy was indeed a vigorous, active little preemie. Although the hospital monitored his breathing, and although his parents lived with the horror of the false alarms from the monitor, they both knew, they said, that he was all right from the first. When I handled him at a check-up, he'd start squirming. He'd squirm in my arms until he could actively grab a finger or a piece of clothing, then he'd settle. He'd move until he achieved active control over himself. If I tried to rock or to soothe him, he'd look up at me as if to say, "You can't do it for me. I can and will." He was extremely alert and responsive to voices, to faces, to Anna, to Paul, to Nancy. He exuded a firm sense of competence. As his doctor, I felt the same way his parents did – Billy was all right; he'd make it for himself. No one needed to worry about him.

Family History

Mary was a well-formed baby with big, beautiful eyes – when she opened them. But she spent most of her early days asleep and inactive. She was hard to rouse, difficult to interact with. When she did react to social stimuli, she seemed to look right through you. Her slowed-down responses left those who cared for her with a feeling that they were not doing their part, a feeling that if they could handle her more adequately, she'd speed up, become more responsive.

Hypothyroidism slows down responses and movement patterns and can cause a severe delay in development. This has been called "cretinism," a label so frightening that it magnified the difference between her behavior and Billy's. It was difficult to mother such a baby. Nancy was bound to feel, "How did I do this to her? How can I repair what I've done?" She was a difficult baby to understand under any circumstances.

"From the first, her personality was so different from ours. The rest of us feel comfortable only when we are doing fourteen things at once. Mary's doggedness, her stubborn, slowed-down pace can drive us up the wall even today. It wasn't until you showed us the strength in her complicated, slow style, and how normal her thinking is that we could begin to believe it."

"I was having a bad time in my own life when they were little," said Paul. "I lost my job when they were five months old, and I had to reorganize myself. Nancy was having a hard time balancing the sleepless nights from the twins, her full-time job, and her efforts to give Anna her due. Fortunately, Anna was a brick. It was as if she sensed that we had enough to cope with. She held off having any negative reaction to the twins 'til much later."

"After Mary's diagnosis," added Nancy, "we were all mixed up. We all three, Nancy, Paul, and Anna, sat down and just decided, 'We'll manage it together.' We faced it as squarely as we could. We had already learned that life needn't be easy, but you make the best of it. And we began to make it together. I have always loved Paul as a father for these kids. I'd watch him handle them, and I'd gain strength. He would do half of everything. He cooked, he cleaned, he changed diapers, he fed babies, he backed me up. The struggle worked, and we all feel good now. My sister's illness had taught me how to separate the illness from the person, and I think I've done that with Mary. I know it's there, but I can look at her and glory in her. Isn't she great?"

Having a child with such a different personality was a big challenge for Nancy and Paul. Not only were they up against a medical diagnosis, for which their only recourse was to wait and hope, but they could not react in their usual hyperactive way. Mary not only didn't fit the mold of this active family, but she demanded a whole new set of responses from them. The fact that she was one of a pair of twins accentuated this. Billy fit in with Anna's style, and even at two she was like a mother for him. Paul and Nancy could relate to him easily. Mary was different.

Twins demand a great deal of any family. The feeling that they engender is one of never enough to go around. No mother ever feels that she has enough to give a second child. When two children come at once, parents feel even more stretched. Mary's thyroid condition and her personality exaggerated this for the Cottons.

Billy was always a piece of cake. But that very fact worried Nancy, for she feared that she might neglect him in her concern for Mary. However, as he became active and skilled, it was difficult to worry about his development. Mary still took most of their time and energy. She was not demanding, but she was difficult to interpret. If she had a long sleep, was she sleeping too much? If she was awake, was she on too much medication? Fortunately, the thyroid medication seemed to work well and sped up her progress from the first.

"Until fairly recently," said Paul, "Mary has been two to four months behind Billy in a number of things. He walked at ten or eleven months old. She walked at fourteen months. He was much more active in terms of running around, once he started walking. She was more unsure of herself. She's always been physically less active." (As he talked, his voice slowed down, reflecting his image of this quiet little girl.)

At this point, as if to protect Mary from her father's concern, Nancy spoke up, "But it's an advantage, too. What we've noticed is that, from the very beginning, she would figure out a clever way of putting one toy on top of another to reach something. He would just charge up to it. She has all sorts of ways of avoiding being active, it seems. Instead, she sits in her chair; she pays much more attention to looking at people's faces and looking around her. He was very serious and dour and would run around like mad. She would smile more, but also could be crabbier, too. She seems to have intense feelings. She is the stubborn one. In fact, we used to call her the 'bum' so much that one of her first words was 'bum bum.'" (As she reminisced, she smiled gently.) "We thought twins would be more alike. Even though we knew they were a boy and a girl, we thought we were going to have carbon copies. It's been more like having two individuals born simultaneously. She was the quiet lap baby. It was fun, because she would enjoy sitting there, being cuddled, and looking around. While Billy, you'd have to sort of beg him for a kiss or a hug. He'd only do it when he was really tired. That was the fun of having the two of them, the fun of an active roving boy and a cuddly girl who wanted to sit in your lap."

"Aside from the thyroid problem," I asked, "were you ever worried that perhaps she was too quiet or that Billy was too active?"

"Yes," said Paul. "She seemed . . . not up to par, especially at the beginning. We *were* concerned about Mary. She seemed to have trouble getting her coordination in moving, crawling, sitting up, and then walking. There was a serious question in my mind whether she would ever reach the same point that the others did. Fortunately, it's now clear that she will."

"We were afraid she might be retarded," said Nancy. "That's when you, Dr. Brazelton, were particularly helpful. Because we would go to your office and I would say, 'Look at the difference.' And you would say, 'They look all right.' But we would ask why she wasn't doing things as fast as he was, or following things. Then I remember you told us, 'Look at your first one and Billy. They're like race horses. They're just extremely active.' We realized that we were never scared about that, because we love active people and we're active ourselves. You said that Mary's a different kind of person and warned us that we might look too hard for problems, when it was really her temperament. When that still didn't comfort us or put our fears to rest, you recommended that we have her tested. That did it. When Mary was six months, a psychologist came to the house to do testing and spent a morning here. As she gave each test, we could see that Mary wasn't behind, that she just had a different style than Billy did. She was only testing Mary but Billy butted in, and so she let him try it. I found that very reassuring. Mary was even more precocious than he was in some of the social realms."

"It was really clear," said Paul. "By the time Mary was six or seven months old, she was interacting more with adults and caretakers, even with Billy and Anna. She was very socially engaging and that was heartening, because it was obvious that she was able to figure out ways to charm other people."

"What were your expectations?" I asked. "What did you expect the twins to be, and how did it differ from what Mary and Billy actually were? I think that's awfully important."

"Well, when we were in the hospital," replied Nancy, "I had to stay for nearly three weeks with them because they couldn't come home right away. I remember one day in the preemie units, when Paul said, 'Look at Mary.' At the time, she was sitting in an infant seat and looked like a plump old Buddha. And Billy was like a little mouse darting around. 'You know she's a different kind of person,' Paul said. 'Will she be able to keep up with Billy?' We recognized that from the beginning; we didn't know that there was anything wrong with her then."

Then Paul remarked, "I don't remember that so well, but I do remember comparing her to Anna. Anna had been so very easy as a baby. She had been fussy at the beginning, perhaps, around feeding and a very slight range of other things. But that seemed minor to us. We were active, fussy people, too. We enjoyed Anna so enormously that we wondered how the next child could give us the same feelings as parents. We were concerned that we wouldn't like the twins as much. Actually, it's been wonderful as they got older to see their uniqueness and the pleasure of seeing them together – the three of them. And also appreciating how they've developed differently. Earlier, we thought Anna was active. But Billy has taken that activity to an even higher level!"

Nancy added, "That's where my training helped. I knew things would change and I understood some of the kinds of changes that would take place. That reassured me and made it exciting and interesting. Especially now that they're toddlers. Some of the psychological changes were critical to understand, for instance, when you know that if you go away, they may not want to look at you when you come back. They won't even go to you. It helps to understand about these separation/reunion responses. You don't take it quite so personally. It's also easier to leave to go to work if you understand these things."

Quiet Child/Active Child

OFFICE VISIT

When the twins were about two, Paul and Nancy brought them to me for a check up. As they played in my office, Mary and Billy demonstrated their differences. Billy literally threw himself at a toy. His favorites were the movable ones, trucks or toys on wheels. He would hurtle across the room, sometimes past the toy, and fall on the floor beside it. Grabbing the toy, he'd first cradle it lovingly in his arms, then begin to push it across the rug. In spite of his high activity, a certain sensitivity came through. When he'd finally settled down, he'd look back at us adults to see whether we were still approving of him. I felt all along that there was a tender streak in Billy. He seemed driven by his need to move and to act on his world, but this was balanced by a high degree of awareness of the people around him. He watched his parents for their approval. If he sensed that he was overdoing his activity, he slowed down as if to wait for them to stop him. Or he'd wait for Mary to catch up with him.

Mary was always behind him. She moved slowly. She sat down as soon as she could. She'd sit and rock in a rocking chair, almost endlessly, as she watched Billy move. As a toddler, her gait had been somewhat unsteady, and she walked with a rather wide base for quite a while. She had been slow in learning to perform fine motor tasks and often gave up – to watch and to wait. However, as she progressed into the second year, led by Anna and Billy, she became more and more competent at puzzles, at building with blocks, at turning pages in books. These seemed to be her forte. She wanted to sit and watch, and seemed to be thinking and absorbing as she sat. When she was ready, she would perform an act that Billy had practiced for weeks. While he needed to act on the world to learn from it, she could learn visually.

Accompanying this visual learning was a kind of inner doggedness. She moved at her own pace, reacted at her own pace. She did not need to please anyone but herself. She seemed insulated from the pressures of this high-powered family. I felt it was self-protection rather than insensitivity. She was learning so much visually that she needed to protect herself from the chaos that surrounded her twin and her sister. She also seemed to care less about what her parents wanted. Discipline didn't seem to reach her. Nancy had her hands full in the second year, trying to understand this determined little girl.

Nancy and Paul spoke to me about the apparent gender differences in Billy and Mary:

PAUL   We basically let the twins use the toys that were around the house; we didn't go out and buy different things. Billy's interest in trucks and cars, from the early days on, without really having a heck of a lot of them around here, was amazing.

NANCY   He takes trucks to bed with him. Mary might play with a truck, but he really loves them. He notices them in all kinds of books. Of all the books around the house, those about activity are the ones he would pick. I don't particularly like the idea that they fit gender stereotypes. They almost seem like caricatures of girls and boys. I like the notion that people are more equal at the beginning, but Mary and Billy screwed up any kind of thinking like that. They were *never* equal. As much as I would try to put dolls in his arms, and trucks in Mary's and Anna's, it never worked.

PAUL   Mary's much more interested in putting things inside of other things. She loves boxes in which you drop things through the top, or piling things up and quietly taking them apart.

The Cotton Family

He's much more apt to take something and drag it around from room to room. When he rushes around, she'll go after him. They do engage with each other in certain ways. But it's striking how different they are.

DR. BRAZELTON Do Billy and Mary fit the stereotype in other realms? In the way they react to others, doesn't Billy seem to fit the "feminine" stereotype, while Mary is more "masculine"?

PAUL Yes, and now that they're over two, they're much more similar than they were before. They play a lot more together. This is a great relief to us. They sleep in in the morning, or they stay in their cribs until eight, eight thirty, quarter of nine some days. That was absolutely unheard of with Anna. They take care of each other. At last!

NANCY That's the greatest thing about twins. I wake up in the morning and hear him singing, and then I hear, "Mary, Mary, Mary," and I know he's trying to wake her up. Then they'll play for a while. He even figured out how to move his crib over to hers. They sleep in the same room. He'll rock and shake his crib over to hers and then hop in. When we got up, the two of them would be playing away. But one day, they had a fight about something. When we came in, they'd taken everything out of the crib and all the covers were off, even the rubber sheet. They were fighting over one of the sheets, and he bit her. He had her finger in his mouth. And she was screaming away. So we now have the two cribs barricaded so that he can't move closer to her. But they really have a good time. Even as infants, they babbled

Quiet Child/Active Child

back and forth to each other. You'd wake up in the middle of the night and hear the sweet sounds of goo goos and ga gas and chattering to each other.

DR. BRAZELTON   Is there any difference in their approach, let's say to toilet training?

NANCY   Oh yes. Again, Billy is ahead.

PAUL   We'd like to get them trained so they'll be able to go to nursery school. A prerequisite for admission is toilet training.

NANCY   Anna wants to see them toilet trained so they could go to school with her. Anna said to her teacher: "Billy is learning to pee in the potty, but Mary is not interested." We don't really push toilet training that much. But he was always more interested. In the summer, when they didn't have clothes on a lot, we left potties around, and he was the one that picked up on sitting on it. When he produced something, we all clapped. Then one day, he called me over to see the potty. I hadn't seen him do it. I looked down, and there was some poop. Everybody does a clapping routine. All of a sudden, we looked more carefully. He'd gone and got a pebble and put it in. It was fake poop, which Mary and Anna both thought was a riot. Mary will not be toilet trained until she feels like it. And who knows how old she'll be at that point! She does things in her own time, she is less shapeable than Billy, I think. So I have a feeling he'll come along sooner than she will.

The Cotton Family

PAUL

Right now, when Mary gets changed, she doesn't like to have her bottom wiped. Each time she gets a diaper, it becomes a battle. She draws her knees up. She screams. She bangs her fists. She's being ornery at this stage.

NANCY

She puts her teddy bear on the potty. She loves to play around with toilet paper. We have a game with the toilet paper, putting it into the toilet bowl and waving goodbye. They flush it themselves, watch it swirl around, and say goodbye to it. She thinks that's great. But he'll take the next step when I say, "Well, do you want to get on?" He'll try. And even if he doesn't do it, we'll sort of cheer him on. He's trying anyway. She won't get up there when we suggest it. She'll play around it. But she will only get up on the potty when she feels like it.

At that point, I glanced over at the twins. Mary had built a house and put a doll into it. She was sitting in a chair and rocking, singing quietly to herself. Out of the corner of her eye, she was watching Billy. Billy was running his truck all around the room, "Brooom! Brooom!" Just then he propelled his truck into Mary's house, knocking it down. Nancy jumped to protect Mary's house, but it was too late. Mary whimpered pitifully, and Billy, looking at her guiltily, lashed out at her with his truck. Mary's contentment was a stimulus and a target for Billy. They were locked in typical sibling rivalry. Nancy tried to control Billy, by lashing out at him, but he already seemed to want to control himself. I wonder if he learned anything from Nancy's reaction.

NANCY

It's reassuring to hear from you that Mary is normal. The hardest thing is to see, not what she doesn't do, but what she does do. She is so stubborn. *Mary was putting a sock on a doll.* Look at her go over each of those toes very carefully, very slow, determined. What is her real capacity? *Mary said something to her mother.*

DR. BRAZELTON   With the quiet child, especially, it's important to look and listen.

NANCY   Her language is not as developed as his. On the other hand, if you think about it, she's putting words together. She just talked to me in three concepts. She said, "I'm putting the sock on the baby," which is quite a complicated sentence. The trouble, I think, is that he's talking like a three-year-old already, and her older sister talked like a three-year-old at the age of two.

DR. BRAZELTON   Yes, it's probably the contrast that you're running into. Isn't this a problem with twins anyway? Parents constantly compare them and feel they like one kind of child better than the other. This must tear at you all the time.

NANCY   I don't spend enough time with them alone, separate from each other. *Just then she jumped up to help Mary get something. I stopped her.*

DR. BRAZELTON   Just watch, she can do it!

Mary, with her back turned to Billy, had begun to pull her house together. This time she made it even more elaborate, with an arch for a doorway, a back door to the room for her doll to get out. As she finished it, Nancy said, "Bravo, Mary! You really did it!" Mary looked up, smiling. Billy came over to admire it, and Mary sat on the floor, proudly displaying her achievement. I congratulated Nancy for letting Mary get the sense of achievement for herself. That is the most difficult task for a mother who is worried about her baby's development – to allow the baby time and space for exploration and experimentation, the chance to feel a sense of autonomy. Nancy has just given Mary such an experience.

DR. BRAZELTON Hey, Mary, that's a great house. *To Nancy.* My own feeling about her is that she is absolutely on target for a two-years-and-three-months-old child. She is on a different pathway than the rest of you. You have to take time to see the complexity with which she does things in order to see that her brain is working normally. In my experience, the slower, more determined children can turn out to be more artistic, more skilled in certain ways, and certainly more persistent in getting where they are going.

NANCY Another problem is that Mary doesn't show that she's aware that there is another person around. I feel less important to her than to the other children. She is so self-sufficient. Yes, I worry that there are times when I don't like her as much as I like Billy.

DR. BRAZELTON Do you ever feel that you'd like to whack her on the bottom when she's stubborn?

NANCY Oh, yes. Putting her in the car seat is a nightmare. She just won't sit and let me snap the belt. I feel as if I could kill her.

DR. BRAZELTON You feel a need to protect her from yourself.

At this point, I wanted to help Nancy understand her feelings about Mary even better. I wasn't sure that her concern about Mary's slower development was all that was bothering her. Mary's dogged stubbornness and her lack of pliability seemed as much an issue. I mentioned this to Nancy.

Quiet Child/Active Child

NANCY   Yes, I do wish I could change her. It frightens
                   me that I overreact so. I feel so in tune with
                   Billy and Anna. I don't think I've ever expe-
                   rienced anyone like Mary before.

DR. BRAZELTON   I think some of Mary's stubborn determina-
                   tion is a reaction to all the rest of you. She's
                   learning how to handle you all. Now, you need
                   to learn how to handle your reactions to her
                   – without faulting Mary or yourself for your
                   differences.

On another day, Paul and the twins came to my office. Billy
was again actively exploring, tossing toys around.

PAUL   Be nice to Mary, Billy. Billy! No biting! No
                   kicking, no biting Mary.

DR. BRAZELTON   Clearly, Billy is putting on a show. It's no
                   coincidence. He knows we're talking about
                   him. Most parents prize active children up to
                   a point. Have you ever worried about his ac-
                   tivity being too much?

PAUL   Sometimes. He can be playing and, all of a
                   sudden, he'll start to throw his trucks. Did you
                   see a scar on Mary's face? That came from his
                   smacking her with a truck. At times like that,
                   we're concerned about how to discipline him.
                   *Discipline was important, but it wasn't Paul's real
                   concern.*

DR. BRAZELTON   Did you see how Billy looked right at you
                   with worried eyes, as if he knew exactly what
                   you were saying? *I wanted Paul to see that Billy
                   was very much aware of things around him. He
                   was as sensitive as he was active.*

The Cotton Family

Finally Paul asked the question that I knew was on his mind.

PAUL   Do you think he's hyperactive?

DR. BRAZELTON   I think he's a very active child – but not a hyperactive one. Any parent worries about whether an active child is hyperactive, because hyperactive is such a common label these days. "Hyperactivity" means they are not going to get along in schoolwork; they are going to get into trouble all the time; they are going to lose friends, they are going to make everyone miserable. The label is a problem, and in any case, I don't see him that way at all. I think he is more impulsive than hyperactive.

PAUL   How can you tell with a child like Billy if he is hyperactive or not?

DR. BRAZELTON   Truly hyperactive children have no controls. They don't try to build controls, or try to keep themselves under control. They fly apart. They don't look to their parents to see if they are going to intercede. Did you see Billy look at Mary just a minute ago after he'd thrown that toy? Hyperactive children are hypersensitive and hence terribly distractible – one thing will happen off in the distance; they'll hear a noise and they're off. Then they're off again to something else. They are overloaded all the time, and their activity is one way of discharging it. Look at Billy right now. He's sensitive to Mary's upset. His sensitivity to people around him won't let him get out of control. I see him as an intense, very determined boy, but one who is really able to concentrate and be aware of others. He's not heedless in the way that hyperactive children are.

Mary reached for Billy's truck, as if to get a reaction from him. He lashed out at her right away.

PAUL   She provoked him. She knows he likes those trucks. How can we help him learn to control his impulses?

DR. BRAZELTON   I think it's a matter of your showing him about control and his learning control over time. Mary does stimulate him to lose control. He impresses me as being able to sense what he's done. Eventually, he'll learn to hold back. That's what I'd rely on. *Billy's real problem is not hyperactivity, but being two years old and the active one of a pair of twins, the other very quiet – both in competition with each other and for their parents.*

THE ISSUES

My first book, *Infants and Mothers*, addressed the marked differences that exist in infants from birth and, in turn, shape the reactions of everyone around them. Individual differences in the babies are as influential in affecting their parents as are the parents' expectations in influencing the babies. They may be even more influential than is the sex of the child. Child development researchers Stella Chess and Alexander Thomas, in a longitudinal study over thirty years ago, first pointed to these differences. They called them differences in "temperament" and demonstrated that this "style" invaded everything that babies did. They established nine "descriptors" of behavior on which babies could be seen as differing:

Activity   amount of movement

Rhythmicity   regularity of needs – predictable or non-predictable

The Cotton Family

Adaptability	how a baby adjusts to the new and different
Approach	initial reaction of a baby to people or things coming toward her
Threshold	intensity of sound, touch, or sight at first response
Intensity	amount of response to a stimulus
Mood	pleasant, joyful, friendly behavior contrasted with unpleasant, crying, unfriendly responses
Distractibility	degree to which an event can attract the attention of the baby away from what she is doing
Persistence	degree to which an activity is continued even when other interests or obstacles are presented.

Extremes of temperament, as in Mary's and Billy's case, are neither good nor bad, but, depending on particular family expectations, they may be seen as good or bad and can serve to label that child for the future. Soon after birth, parents begin to think of a child as "quiet," slow to warm up, "holding back" in strange situations, "low-keyed," "dull" or "lively," "distractible," or "persistent." If this does not match the rest of the family, or if there has been a family history of slow development or hyperactivity or other problems, parents will ask, "Is she all right – really all right? Does this pattern mean she has subtle brain damage?"

In the case of an underactive baby, or an overactive baby, a new parent will wonder whether that baby is neurologically normal. Parents who have a difficult time with either kind of baby will at times either blame themselves for being inadequate or the baby for being "abnormal."

Soon after birth, a doctor can predict the temperament of a newborn. At Children's Hospital in Boston, we have found that sharing this behavior with parents lets them see that it's not their fault. For example, one newborn, undressed and free, will become upset. She will seem to "hate" her bath, but in reality, she will be reacting to exposure and freedom from restraint. Another baby, in the same situation, will brighten and move his limbs cheerfully.

Studies show that, from their earliest days, some babies sleep as little as twelve hours a day, while others seem to sleep most of the time, except while nursing. Crying and fussing can differ as much as sleeping. Certain newborns will cry for prolonged periods of three to four hours at a time, and there is little a parent can do, except for helping to get up bubbles, and soothing the baby from time to time.

In our society, which values initiative, ambition, and achievement, parents may worry more about the quiet, reflective baby like Mary who waits and watches and takes her time to act. If, like Paul and Nancy, they can take the time to watch for more subtle forms of development – complex use of words, quick but skillful play, or intricate skills with fingers – they may be reassured when they compare their baby with more rambunctious peers. Development takes place at many levels, and these less obvious, less measurable achievements may be overlooked.

Fear of hyperactivity, on the other hand, may lurk in any parent's mind when raising an active child. A normally impulsive, "live-wire" child can affect parents in very much the same way as does a child who is hyperactive because of an underlying neurological problem. But, as I pointed out to Paul, truly hyperactive children have certain extreme characteristics that distinguish them from the normal spectrum of active children. For example, the hyperactive children are almost invariably *hypersensitive*. As a result, they are unable to pay attention to any task for very long. Every movement, every sound, every stimulus, however mild, distracts them, and they have an automatic response to it. Along with this threshold for taking in information goes a low threshold for *motor reactivity*. Such children seem obliged to react with movement. The movement in itself is distracting and disruptive. They lose their train of thought and are off to new activity – meaningless in relation to what they have just left. With this constant motor reactivity develops a kind of heedlessness. These children develop a high threshold for pain and literally run into furniture or doors.

Every effort to soothe or interact with them results in an overreaction. In an effort to control themselves, hyperactive children may develop repetitive acts such as rocking, headbanging, or similar autisms – often with a wild, detached look in their eyes. These, too, are bewildering for parents who are trying to reach them.

Parents need to understand true hyperactivity as an outlet for a mildly disordered nervous system which overreacts both to incoming stimuli and to the inevitable response to these stimuli. They need to know it is not their fault. They can learn to teach such children ways of handling their own overreactivity and the disturbing overload of this condition. In addition, amphetamine medication has been found helpful for some children.

The great majority of active babies and children are not truly hyperactive. Parents who watch them carefully will see that they are able to concentrate and have inner controls which will become more effective in time.

Meanwhile, there are a number of simple measures which parents can use to soothe a restlessly active child. For a very active infant, parents can swaddle the lower half of her body before she goes to sleep, or before she is propped in an infant chair. Later, parents can offer a baby a toy to use as a "lovey" for sleep periods. If babies are quieted by extra sucking, I would not hesitate to offer a pacifier, if the baby will accept it and if it has a calming effect. Many active babies profit from extra periods of being rocked and sung to, at times when they are trying to quiet themselves down. This teaches a baby how to break the cycle of intense absorbing activity, and gives her ways to sleep or to move into restful, composed, quiet periods.

When a toddler is upset or in a temper tantrum, a parent could take that child gently into a rocking chair, hold her securely, rocking her until she subsides. Croon slowly and talk to her when she is able to listen about what she has been through and how she is learning to calm herself from it.

Parents can teach very active children ways to keep themselves in check. They can help a child to stay in one room by concentrating her attention on an event there; they can gradually prolong her attention span by evoking her interest. Whenever she shows a little more staying power, they should reward her with encouraging words. Gradually, she can be introduced to more new situations while under the "protection" of one or both parents, encouraging her to handle the confusion and excitement that the novel situation generates. All of this must be gradual; these efforts at mastery are part of a slow learning process.

COMMON QUESTIONS

QUESTION   How can a parent tell whether a quiet baby is retarded or not?

DR. BRAZELTON   First of all, watch and listen. Does he learn more slowly? When he learns something, does he retain it? In other words, can you see gains in what he has learned? Is he responsive? Is he trying to communicate, to handle toys? If your concerns still bother you after observing him for a while, I'd have him tested. Rather than letting such a concern influence your relationship and eventually pass on a poor self-image to him, I'd let an outside observer evaluate him. A psychological test, even in infancy, can easily distinguish between the style of a quiet watcher and the kind of mental retardation which might lead to slowed-down performance. When such tests are normal, it will increase your confidence, and you will pass on that confidence to your son.

QUESTION   Does a quiet child hold her emotions back? Do social situations leave her feeling hurt, as compared to the active child who is more aggressive?

DR. BRAZELTON   Yes, that is very likely. A quiet child is likely to push her reactions down deep and at more

The Cotton Family

cost to her. An active, aggressive child not only meets a situation head on, but discharges her anxiety and doesn't harbor it. Quiet but sensitive children often try hard to please others in order to avoid strife or disapproval. In the process, they may ignore their own needs, again at great cost to themselves.

QUESTION How can I help my son if he seems to be keeping all his feelings to himself?

DR. BRAZELTON You can give him permission to be stubborn or willful and not have to be pleasing all the time. Even more important is to help him understand how he handles his feelings. If he can recognize this, he'll have the choice to change later on. Actually, his style also has its advantages. Children who try to please people around them get a lot of credit. Adults love to have them around and to reward them. It's with their peers that they suffer more. Other children want a child to react directly and openly. One who holds back makes them feel uneasy or frustrated. Be sure to help your son find a friend. One will do, and if they are alike, it will make the necessary cement for entering the larger group.

QUESTION Sometimes my youngest daughter acts shy with other children. Will she ever fit in?

DR. BRAZELTON Shyness is protective. A sensitive, deep-running child is liable to act shy to give herself the necessary time to take in other children, understand them, and then enter into interactions with them. I'd try to set up play situations where she can take her time. Don't rush or push her. That will just make her feel more

Quiet Child/Active Child

protective. She can't help her pattern. Eventually, she may learn very well how to cover up this need. Hypersensitivity to stimuli can have its advantages in the long run; most artists have it – and have found ways to express it and use it to good purpose.

QUESTION

In our culture, we use terms like quiet and sensitive and passive to describe women and feminine characteristics. Are these qualities found in baby girls?

DR. BRAZELTON

It is more likely that we tolerate quietness, sensitivity, and gentle shyness in girls. Nancy and Paul were certainly relieved that Mary was a girl. "It's OK since she's a girl." Most families would try harder to change this pattern in a boy. Unfortunately, many very sensitive, quiet boys are broken in the process.

Newborn babies do show two subtle behavioral differences at birth that seem to be linked somewhat to their sex. But the variability within each sex is so great that these differences are not strong. As newborns, boys are more likely to be vigorously active, girls quietly active. Also, boy babies, in a visual interaction with an adult examiner, have shorter attention spans with a higher peak of attention and a quick drop off afterward. Girls have a slow build-up, more low-keyed but prolonged attention, and a more gradual drop-off. In response to this, sensitive adults (such as a parent) react more vigorously and quickly to a boy baby, more slowly and gently with a girl. Then, if you add the cultural stereotypes with which all of us function, parents are almost bound to elicit these sex-linked patterns if they are available in the baby. When we run head on into a pattern which won't fit our expectations and our attempts to shape, we become anxious and may set up failure patterns in our boys or girls.

QUESTION   How much do drugs taken at birth affect later behavior?

DR. BRAZELTON   In the past, large amounts of analgesics affected the newborn's behavior for ten days after delivery. Since hospitals are now geared more to wide-awake mothers and natural childbirth, no one gives that level of medication any longer. With small doses, the effects on the baby's behavior are likely to be minimal and short-lived. Maybe they affect a quiet, sensitive baby more than they do a motorically active one, but we certainly don't know that. What these transient minimal effects on behavior may do, though, is influence the parents' *image* of the newborn as quiet and sensitive. Then, they will continue to treat her as quiet and sensitive. In that way, they all play out a self-fulfilling prophecy.

QUESTION   Is there anything I can do to help the motor development of my quiet child?

DR. BRAZELTON   Be sure that you aren't pushing him unnecessarily, and making him feel that he's not adequate. If you fit your stimulation to his tolerance (in other words, watch his reactions closely), you can play with him in motoric ways — walk him, romp with him. Reinforce his activity with quiet approval. You'll find he'll very gradually begin to value motor activity more and more over time. If you overload him, though, you may well turn him off

Quiet Child/Active Child

and he'll just become more stubborn and defiant. It must be on his terms.

QUESTION How can a mother develop better feedback with an apparently listless child?

DR. BRAZELTON First, I'd get her checked over by an expert who understands the difference between a quiet baby and one with a reason for delayed development. If there is a problem, early identification and treatment can make a huge difference, not only in the level of the child's recovery but in the quality of it. If, as is likely, she's just quiet and hypersensitive, your anxiety plays into her withdrawal. She will pull away from you because she senses your anxiety. There are many infants who, for temporary reasons (often stress in the uterus), are hypersensitive to stimuli, such as sound, visual, tactile, or kinesthetic cues. They may need to be fed and played with in a rather quiet, darkened environment. To recognize such a baby, one must watch their faces for a frown or "gaze aversion" (looking away) or feel their bodies for the arching that signifies they've had too much stimulation.

If you lower your voice and speak slowly to them, they'll listen and take it in. If you talk too loud or too fast, they'll turn away or frown. If you look at them but don't talk, or touch but don't rock, they seem to be able to take it in. Gradually, over time, they get less and less sensitive, and they learn how to take in more than one stimulus at a time. If this is the situation for your daughter, it can be discouraging. But there is nothing wrong with these babies, and they do get stronger and sturdier over time. If you understand your daughter's needs, you won't feel so helpless as a parent. We've found that this low-keyed approach works, and you will know by her response.

QUESTION

One of our twins is very active. The other just sits and watches. Then, all of a sudden, he does what the other twin is doing. How can that happen?

DR. BRAZELTON

The ability to learn a chunk of behavior by watching someone else do it can often be observed in twins. One twin is active and often practices doing things a large part of the time. The other twin, who is the sitter and watcher, will suddenly perform the act that his brother has spent days practicing. It doesn't seem fair, but I think the watcher is practicing and learning visually. Often, the watcher gets out ahead in the second year when speech is developing. Then the active one becomes the listener.

QUESTION

My daughter is seventeen months old and very active. I'm wondering when she is going to start talking. Her older sister started sooner.

DR. BRAZELTON

An active child is busy developing motor skills and is often late in developing verbal skills. These children can be expected to start communicating verbally in the third year. Right now, she's probably too busy to stop and talk. I'll bet she gets you and her older sister to do everything she wants without speech. If you really want her to talk, hold out on her a bit until she tells you what she wants. That will push her, but I'd do it subtly and not too often.

Quiet Child/Active Child

QUESTION   How do I keep an active child warm in his
crib at night, since it's hopeless to try to keep
him covered?

DR. BRAZELTON   Don't try too hard. Put him in sleepers which
cover his feet and forget about coverings.
Open the window when you put him in bed,
then close it before you go to bed. Then you
know it won't get too cold at night. If necessary, add a sleeping bag. Be sure he hasn't too
many bedclothes to get caught in. An active
baby is likely to be all over the bed.

QUESTION   I've seen sleeping gowns for babies in the hospital that cover the hands, so the baby doesn't
scratch herself. Since I have a particularly active baby who does manage to scratch herself
often, should I use these gowns?

DR. BRAZELTON   Cut her nails more often, but let her have her
hands to suck on. Babies rarely hurt them-
selves with a scratch. Their immunity protects
them. A baby's life at her age is concerned
with her hands. She can suck on them for
comfort. An active baby, in particular, needs
her hands. If she learns to suck on them, it
will be a great comfort for most of her childhood. The trouble is that most active babies
don't know how to comfort themselves or to
calm themselves down. I would even try to
teach such a child how to use her fingers in
her mouth to calm herself down.

QUESTION   Do you prefer finger sucking to a pacifier?

DR. BRAZELTON   I do. A baby's hands are there for him all the
time. He doesn't need someone to be there to
provide them. Parents always worry about

The Cotton Family

whether a baby will suck his thumb "forever." They say, "You can take a pacifier away later on." If he needs some way to subside, an active baby may well need to suck his thumb or fingers for the first five years. But how many adults do you know who suck their thumbs?

QUESTION   My child rocks her crib madly at night. What can I do?

DR. BRAZELTON   If the noise bothers you, tighten the screws of her crib and put the feet in rubber casters. Otherwise, forget it. An active baby has frustration and energy left over from her rapid learning during the day. During R E M (light sleep) cycles which occur every three to four hours at night, a baby like this will get up on her hands and knees to rock. At the point where she starts to learn to stand, she may stand at the side of her crib and rock it. You can't stop it, but you *can* add your tension to hers by trying to interfere.

QUESTION   My two-year-old desperately wants out of his crib. Yet he's so active that I'll never be able to control him. What should I do?

DR. BRAZELTON   Cribs serve a real purpose. Active children are likely to wander at every light sleep cycle. Unless you want to be up restraining him, don't give up the crib until you have to. Also, since he may soon learn to climb out, put a cushioned mat underneath for him to fall onto. At the point where he really achieves this, you'd better leave the crib side down, so he can climb out onto the mat more easily. Then, you'd better make his room the equivalent of his crib. Set it up so it's safe to wander about, but so that he can't get out of his room and hurt himself while you're asleep.

QUESTION   What if a child is worried about her door being shut?

DR. BRAZELTON   I'd be more worried about it not being shut. A night light might comfort her. If necessary, a chain lock on the door will contain her, but she could still call out. You could go to the door to let her see you're there and available if really necessary. Or, even better, you could call to her and say, "Go back to sleep."

QUESTION   When should I buy a youth bed?

DR. BRAZELTON   I'd always try to stick to a crib until a child won't take it any more – usually by three or four years of age. After that, a regular bed will do. An active child needs all the routine and acceptable "containers" he can get to help him calm himself down. So do you! When you are ambivalent or uptight about a decision such as bedtime, you add to his tension at a time when he can't control it easily anyway. Firm decisions about bedtime will help him.

QUESTION   My two-year-old wakes at six, naps in the afternoon for one hour and doesn't fall asleep until ten, even when I put her to bed at eight. What can I do?

DR. BRAZELTON   Grab all the sleep you can whenever she does. Many active children don't seem to need sleep. But their parents or sitters do. I'd urge you to set up very firm bedtime limits. Insist on a naptime routine, as a break for you. If she doesn't want to sleep, that's her problem, but

The Cotton Family

she has to be away from stimulation. At night, I'd institute a very definite soothing routine before eight o'clock. Then, expect her to go to her room and crib. Whether she sleeps or not isn't the question. Both of you need space from each other.

Sibling Rivalry

❧

OFFICE VISIT

When I came out to the waiting room to fetch Nancy and Anna and the twins, Billy was on the warpath again.

NANCY Billy is certainly more of a discipline problem. It's not only that he's active, but he gets so excited that it spills over. He'll be playing with Anna, and they'll be rolling around on the floor. *Just at that moment, he hits Mary on the cheek.* Billy, what *are* you doing? Wait, wait a minute. That isn't fair. *He hits Anna, too.* Go over there. You know you're not supposed to bite. OK? *She makes him sit in a corner, where he sucks his thumb, watching what goes on.* We are saying "No, no, no" to Billy all the time, and I wonder what message we're giving him.

Mary comes up to Nancy and says something to her.

NANCY He bit half your toe?

Mary returns to her blocks, to play as if nothing were happening. She seems so absorbed in her block building that the world around her might as well not exist. As her mother reprimands Billy, she glances over at him, and I detect a note of sympathy in her glance. It is as if she approved of his impulsivity and identified with it from a safe distance. I wondered whether these two didn't value playing the role of counterparts to each other. Billy's first move after he was allowed out of the corner was toward Mary. He

The Cotton Family

came over to watch her slow play as if she could soothe his over-reactions. I sensed their interdependence.

DR. BRAZELTON   She wins other people over, doesn't she?

NANCY   Yes, very clearly – she's a charmer.

I watched Billy while Mary was praised. He attached himself to Nancy, refusing even to glance at his sister. Mary seemed oblivious, blithely going about her business. But at the pinpoint instant when Nancy hugged Billy, Mary stopped her play to watch her mother. Both children, in their own fashion, are competing for Nancy.

NANCY   I've noticed that whenever she gets attention, he bursts right in and tries to take it away from her. However, she's doing the same thing back to him these days. When he gets something, she goes after it, too.

I wanted Nancy to see that rivalry is not only unavoidable but natural.

DR. BRAZELTON   There's no telling how much she learns through Billy because she watches him so much. She uses him and Anna to catch up. Competition speeds her up.

BILLY   Mommy.

NANCY   Yes, Billy. *Silence.* When you get my attention, you've got to have something to say, buddy. You can't just call. That's what you do, you just call. *To me.* It's a daily occurrence. With Anna, when she was just his age, it might have happened once in a while, but not every minute. Sometimes I think of how much attention he gets, and I worry about Anna as well as Mary.

DR. BRAZELTON   Nancy, I think trying to parcel yourself out exactly with three small children, three small individuals, is almost humanly impossible. I'd advise a more laissez-faire attitude. The most rewarding thing for you, and the most important to them, will be to allow them their individuality and to make them feel good about it. That's hard enough without trying to make everything equal. Allow Billy and Mary to struggle fairly, and to find their own sense of themselves. Anna is already finding her own role as a nurturing older sister. She once had you both, and now she identifies with you both.

THE ISSUES

"How can I prevent sibling rivalry?" is probably one of the questions I hear the most. When I assure a parent that there's no way to prevent rivalry, and, in fact, it wouldn't even be wise if one could, I meet with a certain resistance. But I believe that the most important adjustment a first child will ever make will be to learn to share – his parents and everything in his world – with the next child. In China, this is the biggest issue in childrearing – how to teach only children to care about other people. One would not want to avoid the adjustment that is demanded of a first child. The issue becomes – how do you help him make it with as little pain as possible.

In the Cottons' case, the twins presented an enormous challenge. Nancy and Paul knew that they were likely to become absorbed, even overwhelmed by them. What was to happen to Anna? With all first children, there are difficulties to overcome, and when they are solved, the attachment deepens. Nancy had been comfortable enough to go back to work when Anna was four months old and to combine her work with nurturing Anna. Did she feel she'd really made it with her? Were there residual questions which needed to be faced when she got pregnant with the twins?

Anna made a major adjustment to the overwhelming demands of two new and very demanding siblings. She became like a mother to the twins. Was there an underlying price? She had been as beloved and adored as any child could be – by two parents and a devoted older woman sitter. What did it mean to give up part of this adoration? What was the cost of pleasing her parents with an easy adjustment to the two babies? Some part of her childhood sped swiftly by. When she came to my office with the twins for a check up, she was allowed to hold one while her parents undressed the other. She "became" their parent. She was completely identified with Paul and Nancy as they made the difficult transition to caring for twin babies. She was only two when they arrived and had to grow up quickly. She made a very individual adjustment to the two different personalities, playing on Billy's level, while she mothered Mary through her initial difficulties. She demonstrated pride in their achievements, mirroring her parents.

Identification with parents is one of the factors that moderates the competition between siblings for a parent's affection. There are a number of steps which parents can take to encourage this identification and to help the older child through this important adjustment.

1 When the new baby first comes home, find many small ways in which the older child can help, from bringing a diaper to rocking a cradle. The more the older child can participate in the new chores, the less he will feel excluded.

2 When you have visitors or go out together, make sure the older child is ready for the fuss that will be made over the baby.

Hold the older child, focus some of the conversation on him, and tell her ahead that people get a little foolish about babies, but that they think he is very special, too.

3 When the baby gets big enough to prowl about, make sure that the older child has a private space that is saved from her invasions. Use a gate or a toy chest that the baby can't open. Show the older child how to distract the baby with a toy while he protects his own treasures.

4 By stepping in to make sure the baby is safe from physical harm, you'll make the older child feel more comfortable too, and take away anxiety that his aggressive feelings will get out of control.

5 In quarrels that do not involve physical harm, however, do not interfere or take sides. Let them work it out. The younger child must learn to stand up for herself and the older one must learn to compromise, keep out of arguments in order to avoid creating a triangle.

6 If a child reports on a dangerous activity involving another child, thank him for this help. But for other kinds of tattling, "Alice wrecked my tower," try not to reward the messenger with an outraged reaction.

If a parent realizes that there is no way to treat each child equally, the burden of refereeing endless quarrels will lighten. Try to spend some time completely alone with each child at least once a week. Make sure to praise each child's individual achievements during this time, and refer to these special moments during the rest of the week. If you truly value each child for his own sake, and don't worry about the very different feelings you are bound

The Cotton Family

to have for each, your children will sense this and feel loved and important to you.

COMMON QUESTIONS

QUESTION   What is the best spacing between children?

DR. BRAZELTON   I'd plan a second one when *you* are ready – when you can divide yourself in two, and nurture each of them. No mother ever feels completely ready for that, but I think you know when you can make the best of it – when you can help the older one adjust without too much trauma. Having a baby too soon after the first means that you have two *babies* of different ages. You tend to push the older one to grow up too fast. That's not fair. So if you have two close together, you *must* prepare to nurture two babies. The older one will need to regress, and you must be ready for it. It's demanding to have two in less than two years. After two, they're off the ground.

If you wait until the older one begins to become more independent, as they do after two years, you can depend on her to do a certain amount of her own caretaking and to value this independence. As she regresses with the new baby, you can expect her to bounce back and to want to grow up. So a two-year interval makes it a lot easier. After that, an older child can be drawn into a nurturing role with the new baby. She can identify with and imitate you as you care for the baby. With the rewards of such a "mothering" role, she can

Sibling Rivalry

make it through the adjustment. The wider the gap, the easier it is likely to be.

QUESTION   My two-and-a-half-year-old son torments his eight-month-old brother. What can I do about it?

DR. BRAZELTON   Stay out of it as much as possible. Let them learn about each other without your making it a triangle. By now, the eight-month-old can probably handle the older one. Any mother feels she must protect the baby. In the process, she sets up negative vibes in the older child, who resents it. This increases the forces of sibling rivalry. Most sibling quarrels are aimed at the parent, to involve her. Without her, they are non-issues.

QUESTION   But why do their quarrels get me so upset?

DR. BRAZELTON   The reason sibling rivalry gets to a parent is that she never feels she has enough to give to two children. Since she feels she is neglecting one or the other or both, she will inevitably overreact when they get in a struggle with each other. This acts as fuel. It is hard for a mother to remember that siblings get a great deal from each other and that the job of mothering two need not really be twice as demanding. I think mothers really hate to accept that each child is not completely dependent on them. Children develop better relationships with each other when the parents do not hover.

QUESTION   I have two sons, six and four years old. The six-year-old is starting school and the four-year-old really feels left out. His older brother calls him a baby and teases him. How can I deal with that?

DR. BRAZELTON A younger brother is always going to be younger and you can't protect him from that. But you can make him feel it's a sign of inadequacy by jumping in to protect him. Actually, it's a very good time for him to grow up and learn to be self-sufficient. Since he's living in his brother's shadow right now, you might think of getting him some peers to identify with. This is a time for him to learn that he can master things alone and can learn how to enjoy friends his own age. Find one boy his own age and take them places together. Woo him as a friend for your boy. That will help him stand up to his brother.

QUESTION If I let my daughters work out their quarrels, will that make them more competitive?

DR. BRAZELTON You want them to feel good about themselves. If you have special times with each one, they will not feel they have to compete for your love. But you can't protect them from competition, whether between children or in the world outside.

QUESTION How can a child understand the difference between quality time and quantity time? My older son is upset because I spend more time with the baby, but I try to explain to him that he and I have more fun together.

DR. BRAZELTON This may be his way of working out his rivalrous feelings. Perhaps you could offer to include him in your caregiving time with the baby. You could also prepare him by saying

Sibling Rivalry

that now you will have to go to the baby, and asking whether he would rather go find a friend, or do something on his own, or help you? That clarifies the issue for him and gives him choices. The other thing I'd do is to talk about the special time you'll have with him alone when the baby's asleep. He won't want it necessarily when the time comes, but you can use his refusal to point out how grown up and independent he's getting to be. Don't let him make you feel guilty. You'll have more to give him if you're strong and sure of yourself.

Discipline

OFFICE VISIT

On the twins' next visit to the office, with Anna and Nancy and Paul, Billy reacted to his mother's involvement with me by provocative, acting-out behavior.

NANCY   This is what happens a lot now.

DR. BRAZELTON   Lots of sound and fury. He craves attention and probably usually gets it.

NANCY   It starts when he doesn't get something he wants. He also bites, which worries me.

DR. BRAZELTON   I think biting starts out as an exploration thing. Children try to bite, then they find people react. So it makes them excited. They get so giddy with the excitement they caused that they start biting automatically when they're frustrated or angry or want to draw people's attention. You've just got to say, "You can't do that, and I'm going to stop you every time. Other people are going to stop you. Also they won't like you for it." Billy cares about being liked, about pleasing people; so eventually, it'll sift in. *To Mary.* Is there any chance of your coming up on the table with me?

MARY   No. *She lay on the floor.*

NANCY   That's how she acts if you try to get her to do something that she doesn't want to do. She's almost more difficult than he is. *Mary screamed loudly and kicked out at everyone around her.*

DR. BRAZELTON   Do you ever feel you'd like to whack her when she's like this?

NANCY   Oh, yes. But then I hold back. I'm not sure what to do, and I think Mary's picking up on this. I guess I just don't dare touch her. Mary! Oh, I don't like you doing that.

DR. BRAZELTON   So Mary stakes her territory by scaring everyone away?

NANCY   Yes, even her grandparents. I think they are more intimidated by Mary than they are by Billy. You're right. I'm scared, too.

DR. BRAZELTON   The hardest thing about discipline is the guilt it can arouse. Every time you successfully stop a child, you feel, "Oh, my God, have I done too much? Have I ruined her for life?" But there is no reason for guilt, for the most critical thing we can do for a child is to let her learn her own limits by setting them and helping her live up to them.

NANCY   I agree with you. It's hard for me. I think one of the worst moments I had as a mother was the first time I said "no" to Mary. Even though I knew ahead of time that it was a sensible thing to be telling her, I felt terrible. I felt like I'd murdered someone.

DR. BRAZELTON   Well, one thing you can do for that feeling is to pick her up and love her and say, "Look,

I'm sorry I had to say 'no' to you, but I still mean 'no.'"

NANCY   What kills me is that I'm always saying "no" to Billy. It's like a joke: "Billy, no," "Billy, no." With Mary, I think we let her get away with too much. We've been so glad to see her show a little spunk every once in a while that we indulge her. I should be consistent, and I know it.

DR. BRAZELTON I don't think it's possible to be consistent with any child, certainly not with two different ones like these two. If you tried, you wouldn't win with either one of them. Instead of trying to be consistent, try to react to each individual situation the best way you can and make up for it afterward. Discipline means teaching, and you can't teach in the middle of a crisis. Afterward, you can, by picking them up to hug them and talking it over.

At this point, Mary knocked over a stack of books Anna had gathered.

NANCY   That's a naughty girl, Mary. You are a naughty girl for knocking down Anna's books. I love you, Mary, but I don't like you knocking down Anna's books. Give Anna a kiss, and say you're sorry. *She resisted, and Nancy ignored it. Anna looked forlorn, but accepted it. Billy began to climb about.*

NANCY   Billy, you stay on that mattress. He's discovering boundaries, too. Yes, good boy.

DR. BRAZELTON Being more active, do you think Billy's more of a discipline problem?

Discipline

NANCY   Oh, yes, definitely. It's not only that he's ac-
           tive, but he's very intense. It's not necessarily
           that he's angry or that he wants to hurt some-
           one. But he gets so excited. I get upset. He's
           somebody you can't help saying "no" to. He
           gets into everything. Today, at breakfast time,
           he found a way of parking his cars underneath
           the table with the leaves up. That meant he
           could have crammed his finger into the table
           and hurt himself. When I tell him "no," he
           gets really upset. With him, I have to be more
           creative and find ways to teach him to make
           garages, but not under the leaves of the table.

PAUL   Sometimes, Billy will quickly disappear some-
           place in the house, maybe my study. He'll go
           through a drawer, taking everything out in ten
           minutes. He takes a pencil and begins to draw
           on everything. The others don't do that.

NANCY   We find him dangling from danger spots more
           often than either Anna or Mary.

PAUL   He's also strong enough to hoist himself up.
           The other day, he was in the bathroom. He
           was holding on to the edge of the sink, swing-
           ing back and forth with his feet up off the
           ground. I saw him through the door. He
           slipped, landed – smash – on the tile, banged
           his head. He's relatively bump-proof, so it
           doesn't seem to bother him. But it's very dif-
           ferent from the other two. Mary doesn't do
           that at all.

DR. BRAZELTON   Do you ever worry sometimes that maybe he's
           getting too much discipline? Mary's coming
           off as the good girl, and he the bad boy?

The Cotton Family

NANCY   Actually, we do. There always seems to be something to discipline him for. She's more subtle. You wonder what message this gives him. And yet, he takes it in his own way. He's more easy-going than she is. He doesn't like it when we tell him he can't do something he wants to do, but he's more apt to go off and do something else without holding a grudge. The few times we say "no" to Mary, she's much more stubborn. She has these incredible facial expressions, and she'll just growl. She growls. She frowns. And she won't give up.

PAUL   She also screams and cries, which he doesn't do. You say "no" to him, and he'll usually listen. He'll respond in some way or another.

NANCY   We do let Mary get away with things that we wouldn't let him do. She charms us more. He'll just go do it and get into trouble. But her smile wins us over.

PAUL   Lately, she wants to be taken up and down the stairs a lot. I find it much easier to tell him to go up the stairs himself. When she reaches her arms out and says "Up, up" it's very hard to tell her to climb up by herself.

NANCY   She gets more free rides then he does. She doesn't get thwarted, because she's more un-pleasant when you say "no" and more charm-ing when you say "yes." We probably have to get away from the time when we were so glad because she got more active. We did let her get away with a bit more than the other chil-dren because we were just so happy that she was normal. She's turning into a bit of a mon-

Discipline

ster now, but at least we know that she's active and vital. Now we can face discipline with her.

THE ISSUES

Between one and two years, a child is learning about the world in three ways:

1 Interaction with the physical environment; learning about cause and effect. This is the basis for cognitive development.

2 Learning about the caregiving environment, parents and others, and developing a sense of security about people; learning when to respond in a particular way, because someone is there; learning to trust.

3 Mastering a number of rules, or learning about what behaviors are, and are not, acceptable. Children need adults for this. Learning limits doesn't come easily from within the child.

Discipline refers primarily to how the parent handles that last type of learning, but it is affected by the others. A child who understands cause and effect and who has learned to trust is ready to learn limits.

Why does discipline become a problem? A child is looking for guidelines and wants to know what her parents do and do not approve of. Problems arise when parents teach by using punishment when (1) they are under external stress, and (2) when they lose control themselves. There is some agreement among people who study families that the main problems in discipline occur because the parent doesn't know how to manage routine situations and begins to feel out of control just when the child is out of control. Lack of control is normal for a child of this age, but it threatens the parent. When a child refuses to go to bed, doesn't want to eat, or wants attention when parents have no time, parents can feel helpless. Their own judgment can become uncertain. "Do I have a right to ask a child to do this?"

Children are "programmed" to seek stimulation, yet they also seek restraint from the earliest ages. Discipline from parents is the way they learn about the limits of their capacity to seek and utilize information.

In my book *To Listen to a Child* (1984), I offer guidelines for judging when to use discipline and how to pick the appropriate kind. Two of the most important purposes of discipline are safety and the creation of structure and routine in a child's life. The health and safety of the child should be the first priority in disciplinary situations. There should be no question when a child's health, safety, or the safety of another person is involved. Parents should recognize that these situations demand an immediate response. Children are constantly seeking information about how they can safely interact with other people and their environment. It is one's job as a parent to convey that information and to react with nonviolent sanctions, such as removal of privileges, when that information is disregarded.

Secondly, parents need to establish routines for a child; that is, when to go to bed, how often to watch TV. And, of course, consistency in these routines is a tremendous help to the child as she learns about her own need for routine. If an activity is prohibited, it is most logical to ask the child to stop. But when that doesn't work, a more definite, forceful removal like isolation may be necessary, and may put an end to the provocative behavior.

COMMON QUESTIONS

QUESTION   Is it right to show emotion at what a child has done?

DR. BRAZELTON   It is probably impossible not to. But don't demonstrate power for its own sake. Any indiscriminate use of violence to a child as a demonstration of your potency or control is never warranted. It also provides a model of aggression to the child. Using physical force carries the message that physical force is OK.

QUESTION   If you feel upset, should you show it right away?

DR. BRAZELTON   It's better to let it out and get it over with than to harbor a long grudge. But there are also reasons to hold onto yourself and postpone a reaction. If the parent feels he will lose his temper or lose control and will hurt the child, it is better to check himself from being overly punitive. A calm, sure pronouncement is best. It's impossible, however, not to blow up sometimes. Toddlers will see to that. They have a marvelous capacity for finding your weakest points.

   After a crisis is over is the time to teach about limits. Sit down with the child in your arms. Rock in a chair to soothe her. Then, you can offer comfort for having been through a crisis: "It's hard to be a two-year-old." But also reiterate firm limits. This is where consistency helps – them and you.

QUESTION   What if every day brings a new crisis?

DR. BRAZELTON   Often in the turbulent second and third years, it seems as if your entire life is made up of discipline. Try to change the situation, by using rewards or positive reinforcements. In other words, when they are doing something you approve of, recognize it and acknowledge it. Choose a time to go off for a nice rewarding treat together. This is more critical in teaching discipline than any number of rules or punishments. It may help to break an endless period of provocative behaviors.

QUESTION   At what age do you think limit setting should be introduced so that it is effective?

DR. BRAZELTON   I'd always go by the child and his behavior. Limits are a form of teaching. Toward the end of the first year, after the child learns to crawl, you'll find he'll crawl over to something forbidden. He'll look around to be *sure* you're watching. Then is the time he will begin to "ask for" limits, and he'll be as clear about it as that, if you're watching. If the forbidden is dangerous, you must be very firm and take him away in no uncertain terms. If he persists, isolate him so he'll know you mean it.

QUESTION   Sometimes I hear my child mimicking me as I discipline her. Does that mean I'm too hard on her?

DR. BRAZELTON   This indicates that she is trying to learn everything you are teaching her. It shows how important discipline is to her. She needs to repeat it over and over to really incorporate it. She may also be doing it to tease you with it. One of ours used to sleep in the room next to us. When she was about three, she'd come up to a light sleep at 2 A.M., wake, and then repeat to her doll all of the disciplinary measures, all of the bad things we'd done to her all day. We lay in bed, feeling guilty, but in awe of her accurate memory.

QUESTION   My son knows hitting is bad, but he does it just the same. I don't like to stop him, yet I'm afraid that he could hurt someone in his play group. Is it better to see what happens or to stop it when there's this type of activity?

DR. BRAZELTON   Ideally, it's better for parents to stay out of a play group's activities. You just fuel a child to do more. But you can't let him get too aggressive, either. You can pick him up to hold him after he's hurt someone, saying, "It's frightening to get out of control, and I can't let you hurt Susie. Calm down so we can talk. Susie doesn't like to be hurt like that, and you wouldn't either." One of the best ways he'll learn is to put another aggressive child with him, and let them have it out. I've done this with hair pullers, scratchers, biters, and hitters. The two of them will go at it. Then they'll stop, look surprised as if to say, "Why did you hurt me?" They'll realize it does hurt and never try it again. Don't use too passive a victim; this will just reinforce his anxiety, and he'll lash out all the more. So, it's happening repeatedly, I'd take him out of the group 'til he learns more from another child who is his own speed and is aggressive enough to protect himself.

QUESTION   You make it sound as if it's OK for boys to hit and be hit. Is that true for girls, too?

DR. BRAZELTON   Absolutely. They need to learn about aggression, too, their own and how to handle other people's.

QUESTION   When a playmate comes over to my house and does something that I want stopped, how much is it my responsibility to teach that child?

The Cotton Family

DR. BRAZELTON   I'd suggest that you react to the child as if she were your own, and tell her quite clearly, "I'm sorry, but you can't do that." Hold on to her to comfort and contain her until she calms down. She won't like it, but she'll get the point.

QUESTION   Is it ever appropriate to hit a child?

DR. BRAZELTON   Not really, but we all do it. At times, all children seem to have the capacity to push a parent to the wall. But we also all get scary feelings when we've hit a child, and they're telling us something. We could lose control and abuse the child all too easily. So, physical punishment should always be a very last resort.

QUESTION   We hear a lot about children wanting structure and consistency. Is that true?

DR. BRAZELTON   A child needs particular limits at certain times, but each time is different. Although all of us want to be consistent, it is impossible, for no episode is exactly the same as another. The main thing from the child's standpoint is that limits provide safe boundaries in which he can explore himself and also learn about how to incorporate limits for himself. That's the main job of the second and third years.

QUESTION   In our society, the trends seem to swing back and forth from being very permissive to being very strict. Is one more effective than the other?

DR. BRAZELTON   The fifties were a permissive era, and it was a nightmare. Children were so frightened of themselves. They spent their time, as "spoiled"

Discipline

children, seeking limits. The reason a child seems so spoiled is that she's anxiously looking for limits. Just the way she tests you makes you want to say, "Stop and relax!" Setting limits is the second most important thing you can do for a child – the first is to give her a sense of trust and belief in herself. Discipline helps her recognize the boundaries. Then she can learn about others.

QUESTION   How do I react to the temper tantrums my son throws when he is not allowed to watch television?

DR. BRAZELTON   Stick to your guns. Say you're sorry he's so upset, but your rules are important ones. Comfort him after the tantrum is over.

QUESTION   My daughter has developed breathholding spells when she's thwarted. What can I do to break this cycle?

DR. BRAZELTON   Breathholding spells can be very frightening. As long as you have checked the child for epilepsy, the spells really won't hurt her. Fortunately, they are self-limited, and as soon as she passes out, she'll start to breathe. So you not only don't need help, but your anxious involvement will just make them worse. I'd do your best not to overreact by rushing to her or by trying in any way to avoid them. I'd just treat them like any other temper tantrum – stay out of them until they're over, then pick her up to comfort and cuddle her, saying, "It's really tough to overreact when you get hurt or angry. Someday you won't have to." These spells are a sign of immaturity. She will outgrow them.

The Cotton Family

QUESTION   I have a three-year-old who, when something has occurred – for instance, a bowl has been broken — blames it on Joe, his imaginary friend. He's obviously lying, but I'm not sure how to handle this.

DR. BRAZELTON   There's nothing as wonderful as a child's imaginary friends. Treasure them, and realize that he's trying to handle his guilty feelings that way. You must admire his ingenuity. All children go through phases of lying, stealing – almost all the bad things you can name. Imaginary friends in the third, fourth, and fifth years are part of a fertile imagination. Take them as such, and don't overreact. Just say, "You and I know Joe can be a bad boy, but he doesn't need to feel quite so guilty. I'm sure he didn't mean to break the bowl, so he can tell me the truth if he wants to." By accepting his projection onto Joe, you have a chance to play his game, and still put over your message.

QUESTION   Rushing my daughter often precipitates opposition. What can I do when she's late for day-care and me for my job?

DR. BRAZELTON   When it's really very critical, don't give her a choice. Just pick her up wordlessly to dress her. Bundle her into the car and take her. Next time, I'd try to allow more time, so that you can both participate in the important struggles of decision making and of choices. It's a pretty important stage of her development.

QUESTION   Why do temper tantrums occur?

DR. BRAZELTON   They nearly always occur when the child's own ability to make a decision emerges. They are a symptom of burgeoning independence. With this comes a strong desire to make his own choices and *not* to conform any longer to yours. Hence, they're expected when you make a choice for the child. The ones that surprise you are those that occur for no observable reason. He may be trying to decide whether to go in or out of doors, and no one cares but him. He'll lie down in the doorway and dissolve in a rip-roaring tantrum. He's caught by his own ambivalence. Whether or not to say "yes" or "no" – to go or not to go – all of this looms very large in the second year as he learns about his own independence. Your best course is to stay out of the tantrums and let him handle them for himself. If you try to help or to stop them, you are most likely to prolong them. Remember that he's fighting for his own independence. Leave the room, come back after it's over, pick him up to comfort him, saying, "This feels awful, but soon you'll know what you want to do."

QUESTION Sometimes I get enraged at my child. I give her lots of attention, read books, play games, but that never seems to be enough. She always whimpers for more. What can I do?

DR. BRAZELTON No child ever gets enough. She's just testing your limits. Your indecision keeps her fueled. Decide for yourself when it's enough and stick to it. It'll be easier for her.

The Cotton Family

The Cotton Family Revisited

When I visited the Cottons at home, Anna, now a very outgoing six-year-old, met me at the door. She helped her mother as a hostess. She made me feel welcome and at home. She went out to the kitchen to bring in the tea things that her mother couldn't manage. Her movements were quick and adroit like her mother's. She has absorbed her mother's warm friendliness. She looks like Paul with her black hair, her piercing bright eyes, and her charming, mobile face. She is a wonderful combination of these two outgoing, actively successful people. Her mother said she is very popular, and one can see why. Every child must wish she could be as charmingly competent as Anna is.

The twins were the biggest surprise. No longer are their differences so apparent. They are more alike. They are constantly aware of each other, and they behave more like each other. Billy has calmed down. Although he is still quick and impetuous in his movements, he is quieter. He is aware of everyone, and has the same quality that Anna shows, of wanting to please people around him. He, too, helped his mother as she pulled together tea for my visit. His body is compact, athletic-looking, but he no longer conveys the restlessness or impulsivity that he demonstrated two years ago. He is not distractible or uncertain.

Mary is much quicker now. She no longer only sits and watches. She follows Anna and Billy with her own attempts to be helpful. She is still a bit clumsier than they, but it is no longer such a contrast. She is graceful, feminine, and her beautiful eyes are set in a round face with pretty, soft brown curls surrounding it. She watched me as if she, too, wanted to be sure I felt at home. She, too, has grown up considerably. No one hovers over her. Paul and Nancy seem to be sure of her and her development. And, indeed, they are right. She is a well-developed four-year-old.

After we sat down, Nancy and Paul discussed their last two

years and also told me more about the times just before the twins came. Paul had lost his job and had to find another. He'd had to search for it and had landed in an important administrative post. But it was an unsettled time for him. Nancy's mother had died. Her sister's death after a long struggle with mental illness had both depleted and frightened them all. Nancy felt bereft. As she talked, her seriousness reflected her effort to keep it all together. She talked more about her attempt not to identify Mary's potential struggle with her sister's struggle. She had coped with many fears about Mary.

Mary is on thyroid medication and will be for the rest of her life. Her bone age is monitored by X-ray every year, and she is evaluated by IQ testing each year. Once again, I assured them of my conviction that we caught her hypothyroidism so early that there was no residual damage to her brain. We have had her tested repeatedly to back us up, and every expert agrees with us. By seeing that she continues to test high on all cognitive tasks and is now catching up with her precocious, driving brother on motor tasks, her parents are gradually learning not to worry.

Nancy then added, "It was a blow to produce a baby that I feared I might have damaged. I couldn't – and I still don't – understand how it could happen."

I agreed. "No one does, of course."

"Is it genetic, by any chance?" Nancy added. "There's no one in my family with this condition."

"No one knows that it is," I replied. "Do you still feel you treat her differently because you feel responsible for her illness?"

Both parents quickly nodded. "Oh, sure," said Paul. "We feel so overprotective. But we work hard not to let it affect the way we treat her."

I commended them on this, for they could certainly be dominated by such deep-rooted fears. Of *course*, they will always wonder, fear, and even overcompensate. But being aware as they are of their fears and their own personal reasons for their fears will surely help them. Freeing Mary up to be her own person has been a real triumph for them, and I told them how much I had admired the way they'd been able to do that. For Mary is a self-assured, determined little girl who shows plenty of ego strength. She does not expect to fail. She hardly seems aware of her troubles.

I asked how the twins had been able to change so much over the past two years. Mary is much more fun and cheerful. Billy has learned restraint. He still watches to see whether he's behaving properly in your eyes. Mary isn't self-conscious, but she has become aware – especially of Anna. She seems to follow Anna's every move and certainly looks to Anna for direction.

Nancy said, "Anna has done a lot to change them. She really devotes herself to them when she's home. Not that she doesn't have friends and interests of her own. She certainly does. But it's almost as if she were their mother instead of me. Do you think she feels that because I work full-time she needs to do more?"

I didn't comment on that, but I noticed how actively Anna tried to direct the twins. The interesting thing was that they didn't seem to object to her directions. If Nancy urged them to do something, they might do it but they might not. By contrast, they seemed to want to please Anna, and I didn't see them rebel or fight with her.

"Well, we really like rambunctious kids," said Paul, "so you can see how Billy came about. I think Mary has just picked up steam over time in an effort to keep up to him."

"She's still stubborn," added Nancy, "and we don't know when it's that or when she just doesn't understand. He's so direct and open that you know when he doesn't get it, but she's harder to read. She has a real flair for covering up what she doesn't understand. She gets charming and winning on the surface (like Anna), but there's a real stubborn streak underneath."

I asked, "Do you think you still worry about her future?"

They both answered almost too quickly, "No! Not any more. Ever since she caught up to her motor development," said Nancy, "then in her speech, we haven't worried."

"Caught up with what or whom?" I asked.

"With him, of course. I guess she's really had to learn to be like him to prove to us she's normal. I never realized that before."

"They are so dependent on each other," remarked Paul. "They divide up a task. He says, 'You do the gate. I'll do the door.' And

The Cotton Family Revisited

they do. They help each other out. He waits at the door for her. He's there in half the time she takes, but he waits for her."

As they told me about the twins' interdependence, I couldn't help but compare it to the wonderful interdependence of Paul and Nancy. The twins had a fine family pattern to follow, and they took advantage of it. Nancy and Paul were justifiably proud of their ability to overcome their difficulties. It was clear that they were all the stronger for it. So were the children. In this closely interdependent family, everyone relies on each other for support, for fun, for the ability to face life squarely.

The Mazza
Family

❧

CHAPTER II

The Mazza Family

The Mazza Family

Family History

è

Linda Mazza is a single mother of two sons, Christopher, seven, and Andrew, four. They live in a peaceful rural suburb, with woods and fields surrounding the house. Linda works full time as head nurse in the operating rooms of a nearby hospital. When we first met, Linda told me that she'd recently been divorced and that she and her two boys were still suffering from the effects. Christopher was managing well now, but she and Andrew needed my help. She had also told me earlier on the phone that she had only a few friends to turn to. Her family did not live nearby and, while her ex-husband did, he was, as she said, a "constant threat." Her in-laws helped her all they could, but she needed to talk to someone who had some distance from the situation. I urged her to come to my office for a consultation. I told her I wanted to get to know her better. "Should I bring Andrew?" "Oh, yes." I wanted to meet him, and I wanted him to know me, if I were to help them.

Linda, a tall, delicately structured woman, stepped into my office like a princess. She is soft-spoken and gentle. She speaks with sincerity, and gives the other person the impression that he is the most significant person in the world to her at that moment. As I talked to her, it became apparent to me that, most of all, she wanted to be approved of and respected. Her regal appearance belied this childlike quality. As she talked about her boys, her large brown eyes softened, and I could tell how much a part of her they were. She seemed almost to cradle them in her arms as she spoke, a gesture that told me how she thinks of them – as her babies, even though she values them as the independent people they are now.

Christopher, she said, has become nurturing and fatherly toward his younger brother. He is athletic and admired as a leader in his class. Linda's main concern seems to be Andrew.

Andrew, rather tall for four, is a gentle boy with big brown eyes just like his mother's. Deep and liquid, they revealed a kind of suffering as he watched his mother's every move. This appealing dependency was what kept Linda so close, of course, and it is no wonder that she was caught up in it. In fact, it seemed to me that he almost used it consciously. Only as he moved away did his expression brighten and become more assertive. His whole body took on a firmer, more grown-up attitude when, no longer clinging to his mother, he played with toys or interacted with the other children in the waiting room.

With me, Linda's voice was direct and earnest. But it changed when she spoke to Andrew. Her pitch went up a half octave, and she reduced her vocabulary to an almost infantile level. Her baby talk indicated that she thought of him as younger than four. This disparity in Linda's behavior caused me to watch him more carefully. I wanted to see if in fact he really was delayed in his behavior. But nothing I saw indicated it. Rather, his behavior only confirmed my suspicion, that he acted differently only when he was near his mother. For example, he would regress, sucking on his thumb, whining and talking baby talk. Outside the room he stood straight and tall, his expression serene, and he played competently with the toys. It was as if there were two entirely different small boys. As Linda began to talk to me, I could understand this pattern of mutual clinging.

"My divorce came four years ago," she said. (It was revealing to me that she had called her divorce "recent.") "I knew as soon as I had Andrew that our marriage was over. My husband had become angry, even abusive. I knew he felt guilty that things were not working out and that was what made him react that way. But I still felt afraid of him, of what he might do to the children. It was unreasonable, I know. He loves the boys, and he is still a good father. But I felt so devalued and so much a failure. I couldn't stand to be verbally abused like that. Our marriage had to end. If he could treat me that way, at the time of a new baby, there was no hope for us. I realize now that he always treated his mother with disrespect, and in retrospect I should have known how I'd be treated. But I loved him, and I thought he was strong. I needed a strong man, and I had always wanted a normal home. I'd grown up with a mother who was in a wheelchair with multiple sclerosis. Our family life revolved around her illness. I always felt different from other kids. I never dared to bring friends home to such an odd household until I got to nursing school. Then, I trusted that the other nursing students would understand. My father was good to us and to my mother over the long years of her invalidism, but he never really understood us. He made for himself a life away from his family. I wanted a home. I must have known our marriage was falling apart long before, but I couldn't stand to recognize it. After Andrew came, it was as if something happened to me. I wanted out. I wanted to crawl away with my baby. He was so perfect, so quiet, so undemanding and responsive. A new baby just looks at you lovingly. I needed that. My husband was devaluing me – everything I did was wrong – and I believed him. I thought that I *was* stupid. But having Andrew made me feel important. I could look at him and feel like a person who had accomplished something wonderful. It was this contrast that finally made me aware of what I was doing to myself and to my two boys. I wanted them to grow up to be kind and considerate, to be loving, compassionate. I had to get them away from my husband so that they wouldn't feel worthless, too."

I asked her how it had turned out – "getting away." She said, "I was lonely. We had to make a terrible financial compromise – I had to go back to full-time work and leave my baby with someone else. Most of the time, I didn't feel like a person. My boys became my whole life.

"Christopher was a wild man before the divorce. He was hyperactive, uncontrollable, a real hellion. I guess he was responding to the tension in our marriage. Once he knew we were separating, when he was four, he just turned around. He became a 'good little boy,' and he couldn't do enough to please me. He was so helpful with the baby. At one point he said, 'If I'd been good before, Daddy wouldn't have left. Now, if I'm bad, you'll go away, Mommy.' I was so upset I took him to a child psychologist. I didn't want our problems to harm him."

As she talked to me, her voice became pleading. She leaned forward, entreating me to help her with her two boys. I could see how deeply they had been affected by the disruption in the family.

The Mazza Family

Separation and Divorce

OFFICE VISIT

Linda came to my office with Andrew.

LINDA   What I most want to ask you today is how to tell Andrew what happened between me and his father. I want to say that 'Daddy used to live here before, when you were a little baby.' How do I bring that up? He really hasn't asked too many questions about it but he's talked about families in the neighborhood – mommies and daddies – and I'm sure he feels funny that his Daddy doesn't live here. Where do I start?

DR. BRAZELTON   If you can take responsibility for what happened it will help him. You may well say to yourself 'Gosh, I've been taking the responsibility all this time. What does he mean by that?' What I mean is that a child is going to wonder whether he was bad and whether that is why his father left him. Every time he compares himself to somebody next door, he'll question and devalue himself. It helps if you are constantly ready to say, "Your Daddy loves *you*, he just doesn't love me. He left me but he didn't leave you. Remember, he comes every weekend." In that way, you take on the blame. As he gets older, he may turn on you and say, "You're the one who made me have a family that wasn't together." You'll have to be ready to answer something like that. But meanwhile, you're protecting Andrew from feeling that he was a bad boy or somehow inadequate.

I spoke to Andrew, who had come over to listen and be part of our conversation.

DR. BRAZELTON   Maybe you'd like to hear our talk. Would you? Do you ever wonder why your father lives somewhere else? *To Linda.* He told me by moving over here that he was grateful for our conversation. *To Andrew.* You're such a responsive little boy. You know what else? If your Mommy tells you why your Daddy lives somewhere else, she's going to tell you something that I know is true and that she knows is true. That it wasn't because of you. He likes you very very much. And he misses you. But I guess what he has to do is live somewhere else because your Mommy and he don't get along so well.

LINDA   *To Andrew.* Do you understand that?

As we began to be more specific about the problems Linda and Andrew were having, Linda's eyes grew wider and more liquid. At times she seemed close to tears. She sat very upright in her chair. Andrew hovered close by, leaning over into her lap as she talked. She stroked his head.

LINDA   I'm having a real problem with Andrew every morning in day care. It ruins our entire day. When I drop Andrew off, he can't leave me. He cries and cries. I can't stand it. I say, "I'm going to go. OK?" He says, "No," and seems so little and so vulnerable. When I kiss him goodbye at the day-care center, I think, boy, I wish I could take him with me. If only I had the money to stay home. If only I had a real family. This is his first experience with going there, and he seems to stay by himself for a long while at the beginning. It takes him time to make friends.

DR. BRAZELTON   But playing with other children will be the most important thing he can do. In this way, he'll learn about himself, about how competent he is, about how independent he can be. Play is a child's most serious business. This is how children learn about themselves and test their world. Andrew is an able little boy, but he isn't sure of that. He shies away from his peers, almost builds a wall around himself because he's not sure.

LINDA   He almost lets himself be friendly with the kids. They try to make friends with him, but he kind of scares them off.

DR. BRAZELTON   Is he frightened of the kids?

LINDA   I don't know. part of it is that he doesn't want to share with them. I really don't have the answer to it. It's easier for him being with adults.

DR. BRAZELTON   I was just going to say that. It is hard to imagine him being aloof with adults, because he's so good with me. You're absolutely right that a child can be easy with adults or even with older kids, like his brother and his age group, and still have a tough time with his own peers. Christopher is so nurturant with him, so easy with him, that he probably spoils him and lets him get away with murder.

LINDA | I feel maybe that I don't help him enough. Maybe I should push him to play with other kids? *As she spoke, she literally cuddled his head in her lap. Andrew dug in.*

DR. BRAZELTON | A child resists separation in three classical stages. First, by protesting. Then he shows a kind of despair. Finally, he withdraws into himself. *Andrew was obviously using his protest to hold onto Linda; he knew it bothered her.*

LINDA | He seems so isolated. At home, Christopher has taken over the role of Daddy, which I try to get away from. He seems to sense that that's what he's supposed to do, even though he's just a little guy. It's very difficult to play Mommy *and* Daddy. After I work all day long and then come home with the kids, it's wonderful. And then they're naughty. I don't want to holler at them all the time because I've been gone all day long. It makes it so hard.

DR. BRAZELTON | Maybe you need a bit of leeway right now. Maybe your hurt is so deep that you have to give way to it.

LINDA | It's complicated being both Mommy and Daddy. I remember the first time I walked into the bathroom and saw Andrew putting on make-up, I felt panicky. What am I doing wrong? It scared me to death.

DR. BRAZELTON | Tell me about yourself, Andrew. Have you got a friend?

LINDA | Have you got some friends you can tell Dr. Brazelton about?

The Mazza Family

DR. BRAZELTON Who is your best friend?

Andrew clung mutely to Linda to make her take over, to be sure she was involved.

DR. BRAZELTON Tell me, who's your best friend?

ANDREW Karen.

DR. BRAZELTON Karen. She's your friend. That's good. Any boys that you play with? *Andrew shook his head.* Does Karen go to your house sometimes?

Andrew watched his mother as if she were listening, judging.

DR. BRAZELTON I see, so you're not going to say? *But I knew Andrew was listening.* You know what? I think you're leaning on your mommy.

LINDA That's a very good point, really, because I think it's okay for little girls to act like this, kind of shy and behind their mothers; but for little boys to do that, it's our society really – it's not accepted for little boys to be shy and behind their mommies.

DR. BRAZELTON Andrew is under enormous pressure.

LINDA I think that maybe he's used to playing with girls because the only one his age in the neighborhood is a girl.

DR. BRAZELTON It's better to have one friend than none; that's a good sign, really. But I think he feels a lot of pressure. Everybody expects a lot from him, and he's not quite sure what they're expecting. He's trying to live up to it, but he doesn't know quite how.

Separation and Divorce

LINDA   That may be.

DR. BRAZELTON   Here in the office, he seems to regress into
                 being a baby. Does he know that that bothers
                 you?

LINDA   Yes, he does act like a baby at times. It does
                 bother me. Christopher's so grown up. That
                 puts pressure on Andrew, too.

I reassured her that there were worse things than letting Christopher set an example for Andrew. Andrew wasn't learning anything by being allowed to retreat into babyhood and Christopher wouldn't let him act like a baby.

LINDA   But he's not learning how to play with kids
                 his own age. He's just learning to deal with
                 Christopher and me. He seems to feel safe
                 with us. *Linda's eyes showed concern.* At day
                 care, he seems to need direct attention from
                 someone. When the kids come over and try to
                 get him to play, he pulls away. He gets un-
                 happy and he withdraws. That scares me.

Andrew was now shaking a toy in his mother's face so she couldn't see or talk to me. She was dodging back and forth to try and see me, letting herself be manipulated.

DR. BRAZELTON   He's rattling this so we can't talk. Why do you
                 think he's finding it so difficult?

LINDA   I think he doesn't like to be separated from
                 me.

With this statement, Andrew began to be really obnoxious, rattling the toy, climbing up in her lap in a very aggressive manner. It was obvious to me that he wanted to be stopped. While he wanted her to stop talking to me, to pay attention to him, he also,

The Mazza Family

I thought, was trying to establish the fact that he was a person, not an object or a baby. He wanted to be stopped in no uncertain terms. Having to stop him would not only bring his mother back to reality, but would also force her to see him as an independent person. That seemed to be his major goal.

DR. BRAZELTON   Linda, Andrew is telling us something about his own conflicts. He's trying to distance himself while remaining close. He needs to be treated as a person all his own. *To Andrew.* Andrew, you know what I wish you'd do? Would you go outside and play for a little while while I talk to Mommy about some things?

ANDREW   Yes. *He looked at me dutifully, maybe even with relief.*

DR. BRAZELTON   I know you'd rather be here, but Mommy and I need to talk. You're getting to be a pretty big boy. I'll go with you to the door. We'll be out to get you in a minute, OK? Knock if you want us.

He left without a murmur, or without even looking back at Linda. The incident spoke volumes, certainly about Andrew, but more about Linda.

DR. BRAZELTON   Do you think you worry about separating more than he does?

LINDA   Maybe I do. I keep trying to understand what he's thinking. But my own feelings get in the way. I miss him so much myself. When I'm at work, I'm so afraid he won't be OK.

DR. BRAZELTON   Do you remember what you told me about your own childhood? That you always felt as if something were wrong with you because you had such an odd household? Do you think you might be feeling that way about Andrew – that he's not quite up to all of this?

LINDA I never thought of it that way. But I do feel as if I'm a failure *again*. And maybe I include Andrew in that. Maybe I'm afraid that he will feel like a failure. When he looks at me with those eyes, I melt. I feel he needs all I've got to give him.

DR. BRAZELTON But maybe your fears are reinforcing a feeling in him that he can't cope. If you hover, he can't learn how to manage for himself. He seems very able to me. He may need to know that you feel he can manage. If you pull away a little and show your confidence in him, he'll be more confident.

LINDA Am I really holding him too close? I guess I knew it – that's why I came. I need him more than he needs me. But he acts so miserable when we are about to separate.

DR. BRAZELTON I wonder if he doesn't pick up on this from you, if he doesn't sense how badly you feel about going away? Then he plays on that by acting miserable and withdrawn. One of the messages you may be giving him is that he's not able to be on his own, that he's not an independent person. You know, when I asked him to, he went out very easily. He went right out of the room, on his own. I could sense that it was hard for you to believe. The way he did it was so bold and secure. It made me feel that it might be more your problem in letting him go than his problem in leaving you. Could that be?

LINDA   I feel so badly about leaving him that I'm probably making the situation worse than it is.

DR. BRAZELTON   Not worse; I don't see it that way. But I think that if you feel he's vulnerable, or different, or whatever, he's going to pick up on that.

By now, Linda was leaning forward on my desk, hanging on to my words. I sensed that I was safe in saying these rather harsh words to her, although we really didn't know each other that well. I felt encouraged by her to pursue this line.

DR. BRAZELTON   First, you have to understand your own feelings. As you talk about it right now, your eyes get sort of teary. He means something very special to you. I'm sure it has to do with the time when he came along, just before your divorce. He helped you through that time and now you have to learn to let go of him. When you have to leave him, those dark days come bubbling up to the surface in a way that's very hard. Separation is tough for a child, but it is also terribly difficult for a parent. If you can handle your side of it, he'll be able to do his part. So it is critical that you begin to see him as independent or brave or whatever he needs to feel. The fact that you can talk about it here with me means that you both are on your way. *At this point, almost on cue, Andrew knocked at the door to come in.*

LINDA   Your mom's still here.

Separation and Divorce

DR. BRAZELTON   Did you get lonesome? You were so good to stay out there. What were you doing?

ANDREW   I made a big castle. I put the baby in it.

I went outside to see what he'd built. It was a castle indeed, a high wall all around the little baby doll.

ANDREW   Made a castle.

DR. BRAZELTON   What's going in the castle? Are those trucks going in?

ANDREW   No, just witches trying to get in.

DR. BRAZELTON   Witches? What kind of witches? Bad ones or good ones?

ANDREW   Good ones. *He mumbled something to me about what the witches had said. All I could make out was: "They bring spells on the little boy."*

DR. BRAZELTON   Spells, hmmm. Is that what they do?

ANDREW   They take the little boy away.

DR. BRAZELTON   Where are they taking him?

ANDREW   To the castle.

DR. BRAZELTON   Into that castle? What do they do with him then? *At that point, it was as if I'd gone too far; he pulled away.* Don't want to answer that, do you? Here's your Mommy. *Linda had come out to see what we were doing.*

The Mazza Family

LINDA   Did you miss me? Did you? I was only gone
                 a little while.

ANDREW   Mommy, I made a big castle.

DR. BRAZELTON   *To Linda.* Andrew's wall seems self-protective.
                 Inside a private fortress, it's safe. You don't
                 have to prove yourself to anyone. You can be
                 a baby in there. They probably don't like this
                 kind of play at school; they're trying to make
                 him live up to his age group. Other kids don't
                 like to see someone their own age regress into
                 babyhood. One way you might help him
                 would be to get a little boy his own age over
                 to visit and take them out together. Do some-
                 thing fun — like take them to the museum or
                 the aquarium or whatever you can do with
                 them, and let them get close to each other and
                 test each other out, while he's safe. If he makes
                 close friends with the boy, he'll enter the group
                 a lot more easily.

LINDA   Mommy's talking to the doctor about your
                 going to school and sometimes how you won't
                 let me leave. Would you tell the doctor why,
                 honey?

ANDREW   Because I love you.

LINDA   Because you love me? Why, I love you too,
                 honey. Sometimes it's hard for me to leave you
                 in the morning, but you know I come back,
                 don't you?

ANDREW   Yeah.

Separation and Divorce

THE ISSUES

Separations are bound to be difficult for the child. After the loss of one parent, he is bound to fear that even a temporary loss of the other parent repeats the first, more permanent loss. If one can leave, why not the other? The remaining parent also feels needy and deserted, and may cling to the child or children. Both parent and child see each small separation, each step in development, as magnified, and a threat to what may be by now a rather fragile balance – achieved after the loss of the other parent. These are the stresses of single parenting. They are not neurotic; they are normal and expectable.

Separating from a child is difficult for any caring parent, perhaps the worst prospect he or she will ever face. Even smaller separations along the way – weaning from the breast, letting the child feed himself, the first temper tantrum – are difficult, even in normal families. But for a single parent, who feels deserted, they are more intense. In Linda's case, for instance, her own needs are so great that she's bound to use the children to shield herself from loneliness, and from the hurt of abandonment. These feelings are communicated to the children. They are naturally afraid to leave her, or to entrust her to the world outside, and she is bound to reinforce these fears. This is predictable following a divorce. Luckily, Linda realized that she and Andrew were stuck, and she reached for the help she needed.

Most parents easily recognize separation as a problem. They know the issues. What is difficult for them is to put the issues into perspective. Linda needed to see that Andrew's own sense of himself was at stake. Pushing a child to be independent will reinforce his own sense of himself. Discipline and distance will give him space, and the permission he needs to learn what his boundaries are. When parents hover, they reinforce their child's dependency and fears. When they draw back, they force the child to rely on his own strengths. This way he learns to cope.

If a child in a single-parent family does not feel competent and able to separate, his own feelings of guilt – over having contributed to the family break-up – may be confirmed. This gets to

The Mazza Family

be a vicious circle, as the child becomes more insecure, more guilty. A single parent like Linda must first recover from her own grieving. When she is strong enough, able to think clearly and intelligently about her children's feelings, she can then make sure that she is not clinging to them for her own sake. A parent may want help with this.

Linda and Andrew had what is called a symbiotic relationship, that is, each fed into the other's needs in a way that was difficult to change. Linda came to me for help in breaking this tie with Andrew. From the things she told me, and from the way she demonstrated her dependence on him in front of me, I could sense that she was ready to change. She and I both knew how hard the separation would be, but I could help her realize how critical it is to Andrew's future.

At each stage of their social and emotional development, children need to test out the questions they have about themselves in relation to the family situation. Divorced parents, still locked into their own grief or guilt, are unavailable, unable to see through to their child's need to ask some real questions – about himself. That's why it's critical for divorced (or widowed) parents to get on with their own adjustment. Otherwise, they do not hear his pleas, they project their own struggles onto the child (by reinforcing the sense of responsibility he inevitably feels), or they infantilize the child (to protect him, to hold him close – but not in his best interest).

Most single mothers enter the work force after a divorce. For them, all of these issues are doubled. First of all, they feel angry, overwhelmed by their new situation, and may well long to be free to stay home with their child. They react to this anger by being overprotective, ambivalent about leaving the child with a caregiver. These reactions, in turn, are conveyed to the child, who struggles against being left. Work can be a salvation of a kind for a single parent – peer contact and support, a chance to meet others, a confirmation of worth. A single parent sees it as a step toward her own independence. But it can have the opposite effect on her relationship with her children. It may make her cling to them, and vice versa. Nevertheless, any job can be a positive force in preparing a parent to let go.

All parents need to know when their child needs a push, when he needs discipline, when a problem is his, and when it's hers. Being a single, working parent simply clouds the issues. There is no other person nearby to give her a proper perspective on her situation. Seeking help can be a sign of strength, a readiness to make a positive adjustment.

JOINT CUSTODY. Linda Mazza has full custody of her two children. Many divorced couples work out an arrangement of joint custody. Then, the threat to the child is something different, not loss of a parent, but loss of a sense of territory and of identity. The following guidelines may help parents safeguard their child's sense of place and belonging, which is a critical part of his development:

1 In each house, be sure the child's room is not changed or shared without his permission. Talk of it as *his* room. If he needs to share it with step-siblings, remind him that it's his bed or his corner.

2 Be sure he has a special "lovey" or toy that he can take back and forth between the two houses. This gives him a sense of continuity. If he has a sibling who shares joint custody, it's a hundred percent easier. They will learn to rely heavily on each other.

3 Have definite times when you pick them up and when you take them back. Stick to these times as carefully as possible, and apologize when you don't. A calendar marked with red and green for the days spent in each house will help.

4 Don't fight with each other as you take the child back and forth. Save it for another time. Every switch is a wrench for the child, and that needs to be respected.

5 Allow for a temporary regression after each switch. Allow the child to be cuddled "like a baby," and even explain this to him after you switch. It will help him understand himself.

The Mazza Family

6 The more routines you and your ex-husband can agree on, the more it will help in the switch. This is not to say that two very different people can, or even should, treat their child alike. Not only is it impossible, but it would come across to the child as hypocritical and shallow. A number of similar routines are reassuring to a child who is searching for something stable in a constantly changing environment.

7 Above all, it is critical to the child to know that both of you care about him *and* understand him. If you are indulgent whenever he is with you, he will feel that you are only dealing with part of him. Children value discipline. They need limits as much as they need evidence of positive caring. But most of all they value a parent who deeply understands what they are going through and who communicates that understanding to them. When the child is with you, each of you must be a parent at all levels.

The life of a child in joint custody can be difficult. But if the parents are able to follow most of these guidelines, the child has every chance to grow and flourish.

COMMON QUESTIONS

QUESTION What about a mother who is widowed? How can I keep from burdening my baby with my grief?

DR. BRAZELTON The grief of losing one's husband, with a baby to raise, must be enormous. Of course, some of the grief will be felt by the child. In grief, a person is slowed down; eating, sleeping, everything is more difficult. The widowed parent may well cling to the child for consolation. This can be a real salvation for both. Even though you may indeed be slowed down and not very cheery with your baby, she is getting a feeling of how special she is to you. Your reactions to her will give her a sense of her importance. You are bound to be in a period of self-blame, of anger and self-pity at what life has dealt you, and of denial of the painful reality around you. The sooner you can work out your side of it, the better for her. Babies are amazingly resilient, and can come back from a parent's depression, if the parent can gradually pull herself together to look at the baby's side. The most difficult aspect of being depressed with a small baby is that you haven't the energy to respond to *her* and to her leaps in development. Often widowed parents will seek help and support, to be ready for the rebellion and separation that all parents face.

QUESTION

How will I know if my son thinks he's the cause of my divorce?

DR. BRAZELTON

If you are alert to the strong possibility of his feeling this way, sooner or later you'll hear him try a sentence like, "Do you think Daddy likes me?" If you say, "Of course he does, why do you think that?," he'll give you some answer to change the subject. If, on the other hand, you say, "Do you worry about that a lot?," he might answer, "Well, he doesn't come around very much." Then you could say, "Do you ever worry about whether you were the reason for our divorce?" He'll say "no" with his head, but he'll look at you with "yes" in his eyes. Then you can say, "All kids in a divorced family worry about whether they caused it by being bad, or by doing something that their father didn't like. It's not true, you know. Your dad loves you no matter what happens. He doesn't come around because he doesn't love me any more. So we had to live apart. It's hard on you, for it makes you worry. But it's not your fault. I hope you can tell me when you're worried." This last sentence is important because the subject will need to come up over and over, in many different guises.

QUESTION　Is divorce harder on a younger child?

DR. BRAZELTON　There are different issues for every age. The loss of the absent parent, and the depression and grief of the present parent, will affect the youngest child the most. At each age, a child may regress to a previous stage of development. For instance, the last accomplishment may go, such as toilet training or speaking in sentences. Don't be surprised and do give the child time. Parents can watch this regression as a way of telling when a child is beginning to get her feelings under control. When this happens, she'll begin to take a spurt in development again.

QUESTION　Is a divorce bound to be a traumatic event for a child? After all, nearly half of the marriages in our generation will break up.

DR. BRAZELTON　If you are asking me whether a child can withstand the breakup of a family, my answer is "yes." But parents must be free and available enough to help the child with his side of it. Childhood is a vulnerable time, and most children who have had two parents continue to long for them and to feel a sense of loss. They may even feel damaged when one of them goes away. That sense can be repaired, can be mitigated, but it needs the attention of adults around the child. A larger issue implied in the same question is whether anything can really replace the two-parent family as a nurturing situation for children. I don't think so. In order to provide a secure, encouraging environment for a child, a single parent must work hard and make an adjustment. Any divorcing parent would like to think the situation doesn't matter to the child. That is wishful thinking, a defense against guilt. It is not the reality, or an attitude that is in the child's best interest.

QUESTION   What about joint custody? Is this the best way to handle divorce situations for the child?

DR. BRAZELTON   I don't know. It seems pretty stressful for a child to be moved back and forth and never to be quite sure where she is. One little girl wouldn't let me enter her room when I went on a house call. She said, "It's my room," as if I were invading something she had to work hard to protect. She was shared, living with one parent three days a week and four days with the other. On the other hand, to have each parent all to yourself can be pretty special. It can make up for a lot of the loss. One danger in a divorce is that the absent parent may grow away from the child. This isn't so likely to happen in shared custody.

QUESTION   What about the parent who does not want a child to grow up like the other parent? Can you tell the child not to act like his father?

DR. BRAZELTON   No, because all it means to him is that he's bad and so is his father. He will need to know what is good about this father in order to identify with him in fantasy. He needs to have a male figure to identify with, so he can separate from you successfully. (A girl needs an image of a father who values her as a female.) I'd talk to him about the good things you want him to identify with. If you concentrate on the behavior that worries you, you give it an importance which could result in a self-fulfilling prophecy.

QUESTION   What if there aren't many good things about his father?

DR. BRAZELTON   Make them up. You want your boy to have a good image of himself as a man. He needs a father image to identify with.

QUESTION   Is there anything I can do to help my daughter when I go back to work?

DR. BRAZELTON   You can certainly prepare for it. Once you know when you will be starting, talk about it ahead of time. Many parents try to slip away to avoid the turmoil of leaving. They may protect themselves that way, but they destroy their child's trust in them. By talking about it ahead of time, you prepare yourself as well as her. Sorting out your own feelings may be the most important part of the adjustment. You can warn her about how long you'll be away and confirm when you'll be back. Remind your child of her "lovey," of the sitter, or whoever will be with her, and how she has handled other separations. When you leave, don't dawdle around anxiously. Get out and let her handle it. Hanging around will only make it harder, and is really a sign that you have a problem in leaving. When you come back, remind her that you told her when you'd

Separation and Divorce

be back. Each daily separation becomes a learning experience and you can congratulate her on her ability to handle it.

QUESTION   Is it normal to feel a little jealous when your child warms up to the sitter?

DR. BRAZELTON   Jealousy is an OK and normal emotion. You can't help but want to have that baby all to yourself. These feelings are another sign that separation is more of a threat to you than it is for your child.

QUESTION   What if a child cries every time you leave?

DR. BRAZELTON   He'll stop when he's ready. One mother told me that her four-year-old son used to cry every time she dropped him off at day-care. The mother asked him, "When are you going to stop crying?" The little boy said, "When I'm not sad anymore if you leave." A couple of days later, he stopped.

QUESTION   How do I reassure a child that I'm not going to die? That seems to be my three-year-old's greatest fear since my separation from her father.

DR. BRAZELTON   It's bound to be a fear in both of your minds. You are now so important to her. I'd reassure her (and yourself) that you won't leave her and that her father did not die. Underlying her question may be: "If I'm bad, will something happen to make her leave me?" Her fear of your death goes with fear that she may be responsible for her father's going away. It's important to address that. The fear is also likely to come back at about four when aggres-

The Mazza Family

sion comes more to the surface. She will need to test out her feelings, and fears and nightmares reflect her anxiety about getting out of control.

QUESTION   If a mother has to work, when is the optimal time to go back to her job?

DR. BRAZELTON   There are times when it is very hard to separate. At any new development stage, weaning or walking, for instance, children are more vulnerable, more needy. Otherwise, separating is probably more your issue than your child's. It will be hard for you to give him up, to share him with another. If you have a competent, caring caregiver at home or in a center, you can be pretty sure he won't suffer too much. In my book *Working and Caring*, I address the issues of what to look for in a good substitute caretaker or a day-care center. I consider the first four months essential for new mothers and babies to get to know and enjoy each other. First-time mothers may need more time. The whole first year is so exciting that it's hard to give it up. By the second year, both of you may be ready to separate. Putting your child in the care of another must be an individual choice, but a choice, nonetheless. The problem for many single parents is that the choices are taken away by necessity. The guilt and longing for the child enhances the problem of leaving him.

QUESTION   Does anyone know whether separation in day care really affects attachment and development?

DR. BRAZELTON   Recent studies show that good day care enhances a child's development; bad day care affects it negatively. It seems critical to me that you find a day care or substitute center that you feel comfortable about. Then, the child is likely to flourish.

QUESTION   When my child comes home from day care, she always cries. How can I tell whether she's had a bad day there or is just cranky?

DR. BRAZELTON   All children save their feelings up for you at the end of the day. That disintegration is the most important message she's got for you, and says: "You are my most important person." It isn't necessarily a message about having been miserable. It's too universal. The only way to be sure about whether she's OK is to drop in at unexpected times to see how she's doing. Don't let her see you; just watch to see how attentive they are to her, whether she's happy or not when you are not there.

QUESTION   But the center insists that parents come only at certain times. I don't want to break the rules.

DR. BRAZELTON   That's generally true, and I wouldn't disrupt your daughter's day very often. But you have a right to reassure yourself. She's yours, after all. So I'd go ahead, and blame it on your own feelings. If the center is too rigid, I'd look for another one. They should be ready to nurture you, too.

QUESTION   My nanny really loves my son and takes good care of him. But she seems critical of me.

The Mazza Family

DR. BRAZELTON   Of course. That's to be expected. All people who care about small children will be competitive for them. So, even a very good child-oriented person will unconsciously be critical of you. At that point, you must balance how good she is for the baby against what your needs are. You may have important needs, too, especially if you're a single working parent, and I'd pay attention to them.

QUESTION   My four-year-old daughter won't let anyone else into our life. When we're together, it's intense. We eat dinner together, we talk together. She's almost more my roommate than my daughter. If I tell her I have a friend coming over, she'll say, "Is it a boy or a girl?" How much should I tell her? I'm nervous she's going to say to somebody, "Are you going to sleep over tonight?"

DR. BRAZELTON   She's become your conscience. Repeated but superficial relationships must frighten a child. If people are only casual friends, there is no need to have her involved. When you have a serious relationship, she will then be more ready to relate to him. If she has to sort out her feelings about one man after another, she will learn not to dare to value deeper attachments.

QUESTION   How should a single father introduce a new girlfriend?

DR. BRAZELTON   Women are often discouraged by the possibility of having a ready-made step-family, so you have to tread carefully there. You also need to be careful of your children's feelings as you parade beautiful, nurturing young women by them. Children of single parents are especially vulnerable, because they need an adult of the opposite sex. They will recognize in each young woman a substitute mother. You can say, "This is a friend of mine and she would like to be a friend of yours." But don't imply or let them think she's here to stay until it's absolutely certain. They may be able to allow her to share you, although they will probably resent it, and you'll have to help them. But there is no need to involve them deeply with transient friends. It is better if they don't learn to depend on them. As I said before, they can't tolerate making intense, meaningful attachment to one person after another without experiencing a sense of loss over and over. So don't do that to them. Don't let them get deeply attached too often.

Sleep

❧

OFFICE VISIT

Linda Mazza came to my office after work. She wanted to speak
to me alone.

DR. BRAZELTON How are you, Linda?

LINDA OK.

DR. BRAZELTON That sounds like not entirely OK.

LINDA Mmmm. One thing that's really hard lately is
getting Andrew to sleep at night.

DR. BRAZELTON Sleep and going to bed require independence.
And I know you've had trouble with his de-
pendence on you, leaving him at school, for
instance. It's all connected, I'd say.

LINDA When he was very little, when I was first getting a divorce, I let him fall asleep in the living
room with me instead of putting him to bed,
which was great at the time. But now that he's
four years old, it's getting to be a problem.
When he does go to bed, he wants me to stay
in his room until he gets to sleep. He cries if
I leave him. He's having an awful time. It's
not so bad when I'm there by myself, but if I
have company I never get him to sleep.

DR. BRAZELTON He has to learn to do it by himself. But for a
working mother or single parent, sleep is one

of the hardest areas. It's a gloomy time of day, and when you are lonely yourself, it's hard to push him to be by himself. But it's also a critical lesson for him. Tell me one thing: does he have a teddy bear or anything he takes to bed with him?

LINDA   He's got a little bunny that he takes to bed.

DR. BRAZELTON   If you talk about his bunny during the day, you make it important to him at night. "Here's your bunny. Remember, when you get pretty upset at night and need something to turn to, you have your bunny. You've got your big brother, and you've got your bunny. You've got a lot of friends near you." And then, toward the end of the day I'd start talking about what you're going to do, to get him prepared for it.

LINDA   Right.

DR. BRAZELTON   What happens in the middle of the night when he wakes up or comes to light sleep?

LINDA   Occasionally, he comes into my bed with me. I try to discourage that, but he does occasionally. But the biggest problem is just trying to get him to sleep.

DR. BRAZELTON   I do think it's critical that he knows that your room is yours and not his. In a single-parent family, it's even more critical that a child recognizes that there is space that belongs to Mommy, and space that belongs to him. A child wants to blend those spaces. So I would urge you to be very sure about your decision at night. Let him know you're going to be firm about it. A child comes to light sleep about every three to four hours, and if you don't make it clear, he will stay awake and try to get your attention. He won't learn to be independent at night.

LINDA   One evening I went out and when I came back, the babysitter said that Andrew cried when I left. The sitter asked him why, and he said, "Well, what could happen if Mommy didn't come home?" The babysitter said, "What do you mean?" "What if Mommy died?" he said. And Christopher said, "Well, Daddy would take us." But Andrew answered, "No, Daddy wouldn't take us." I think that maybe he feels frightened. He feels as if he's going to be abandoned. It's scary for him and it's scary for me.

DR. BRAZELTON   Maybe this is the key to Andrew's sleep problem.

LINDA   I'm trapped, and I feel so bad for him. *She seemed so vulnerable herself at this point, so close to tears. I could see that it was her issue as much as Andrew's, but I wasn't sure how hard to press her.*

DR. BRAZELTON   Do you think he feels your insecurity, Linda?

LINDA   I know he does. We seem to be so much a part of each other.

DR. BRAZELTON   Do you think he cries for help at night because he senses that you are lonely?

Sleep

LINDA   *She pauses.* Yes, I think you're right. Ever since the divorce, I've felt so isolated. Do you think I use Andrew to protect me?

DR. BRAZELTON   Do you?

LINDA   I never thought of it before, but perhaps I do. I don't mean to, but maybe I hold him too close. Do you think I do that at night, too? What can I do?

DR. BRAZELTON   Teach him that he can handle independence during the day first. Let him use his bunny as a symbol. Talk to him about using the bunny at night too. You yourself will have to be sure you mean this. Tell him that you can go back to sleep by yourself at night when you wake up. Then when he comes to your bed and when he wakes up at night, press him to take care of himself. If you're determined and sure, he'll know it.

LINDA   Are you saying this because you feel it would be good for him?

DR. BRAZELTON   Yes. When you come home from work having been away from him all day, I think it's particularly hard not to make the evening go on or to feel that you haven't done enough for him all day. "How can I cut him off at night?" Do you ever have that feeling? *Linda nodded.* Do you have friends that you go out with; people that they know?

LINDA   Oh yes.

DR. BRAZELTON   You might talk about that with both boys and say, "You have your friends, I have mine. I

The Mazza Family

need time to see them." I think it's important to do that because then it gives them some insight into what your needs are, lets them know that you have a life you are going to build, too. Single parents can become so wrapped up in children, in the responsibility, that there's no other outlet. It's good for the boys to see that you need time for yourself. I'd start talking about it at 5:00 P.M., saying, "Remember our routine." Remind Andrew of his bunny; remind him that he'll have to get to sleep by himself. After supper talk about it again. Once he gets to bed, leave it up to him when he'll get to sleep. Once he learns to do this, you'll both feel relieved.

ISSUES

Sleep is a major concern of many parents today. The more frantic their lives, the more likely are their children to have trouble sleeping. And, in any family, at the time of a crisis, children's sleep is likely to be affected. Sleep patterns at night reflect the rhythms of the daytime cycle. When a child is learning something new, when she is under the stress of an adjustment during the day, her frustration or her anxiety is carried over to the nighttime. Her sense of herself as dependent or independent affects how she will handle the job of learning to sleep by herself at night.

Our society generally expects a child to be independent at night. Many other societies, and certain groups within our own, tolerate families sleeping together. Because we expect independent initiative and individualism in adults, helping a child learn that she can manage by herself at night is an important part of childrearing practice. To do this, however, does not mean to be rigid or unresponsive. A child who finds independence at night difficult does not need to be deserted, nor punished. She needs to be supported. Learning to sleep through the night means that, when a child comes up to light sleep (REM, or rapid eye movement), she must learn to scrunch down into her bed, find her own nesting pattern, and then get herself back into the next deep sleep cycle. We all learned this in childhood, unless we are today terrible sleepers. REM, or light sleep, cycles occur every three or four hours. A child must find her own way of self-comforting, of soothing herself back to sleep. Later, when waking up at night is due to motor and learning energy left over from the day, she must learn these patterns again.

If parents work and are away all day, it is much harder for them not to rush in to the baby at each whimper or rustling that signals a light sleep cycle. Getting past these moments is a learning process for the baby, like any other step in her normal development. The baby must do it alone. If parents insert themselves, help the baby settle down, they become part of that pattern, and the baby fails to learn to sleep by herself.

A single working parent finds it even more difficult to separate from the baby at night. The parent's loneliness and need for the baby confuse the issue. How can a parent do this without feeling that she is deserting the child at a time when she needs her the most? Linda's need for Andrew prevented her from even asking this question. Once she was able to separate out her own feelings, she understood that Andrew would feel very proud of himself to become independent from her at night. Being too close to his mother at night becomes even more threatening for a boy, who needs to see himself as a masculine, independent human being. In the period of three to six, when close attachment to the opposite-sex parent is an expectable developmental step, a child who has not already achieved independence at night may have more persistent sleep problems. Without a father around, Andrew has a tougher time assuring himself of his masculinity and moderating what has become too strong of a tie to his mother. Linda must push Andrew harder than she would if his father were around. Independence at night is even more critical to such children than it might be otherwise.

The Mazza Family

COMMON QUESTIONS

QUESTION
My nine-month-old baby wakes up at night, and so I get up and rock her to sleep. It's exhausting. How can I stop this?

DR. BRAZELTON
You are her sleep pattern. You'll have to teach her gradually to learn to get herself to sleep. Rock her, but put her in her crib before she's quite asleep.

QUESTION
Do you believe in letting a baby cry it out?

DR. BRAZELTON
I don't like that concept. A baby needs to learn to feel independent and competent at night, not deserted. One thing you can try is to sit by the baby and pat him. He may go on crying and look accusingly at you, but you can keep saying, "You can do it. You can do it." Do this at naptime, too. Give him a teddy bear to cuddle while you pat him.

QUESTION
My daughter has a whole raft of toys in bed but she throws them all out. She wants me!

DR. BRAZELTON
One toy, singled out all day and at night, is a lot more important than a "whole raft" of un-important ones. By handing a special one to your baby when she cries for you, you are saying, "Here, this will help you do it for yourself." If she throws it out, tie it to her bed with a short length of ribbon, so she can pull it back herself when you have finished the game of retrieving it. *A long cord is not safe.*

QUESTION My two-year-old still gets up twice a night. I understand that I should comfort him in his bed, but my husband can't stand to hear him cry.

DR. BRAZELTON Unless you both agree, it won't work, for a two-year-old knows very well when you are ambivalent. Explain that to your husband and then when you do agree and teach your son that he can manage for himself, your husband will be as relieved as you are. In fact, he'll be proud! After you've made up your mind, it may also help to go to him *before* he awakens the first time. Wake him yourself, comfort him and give him his favorite toy. Tell him that he can have this toy when he wakes up. Later, when he wakes by himself, call out to him that he can find his toy. After he's cried for ten or fifteen minutes (set your clock), then go in to him. Pat him and hand him his toy. But don't get him up. You'll find he'll eventually take responsibility for his own sleep pattern.

QUESTION My four-month-old baby goes to sleep and wakes up at 1 A.M. I take her to my bed to nurse. She ends up staying all night, usually because I fall asleep. Will this turn into a problem?

DR. BRAZELTON It may not be an easy pattern for either of you to give up. I think you'd better make up your mind now about whether you want her in your bed later. She'll demand it, in all likelihood. Somewhere between four and six months, a baby can begin to stretch out to an eight-hour sleep pattern. I'd advise you to wake her around 11, before you go to bed, and feed her. When and if she wakens later, don't rush in right away. That will push her toward a longer sleep pattern.

QUESTION   My two-year-old won't take a nap, and by the end of the day I'm exhausted. Should I force him to take a nap?

DR. BRAZELTON   He may not need to sleep, but he needs a break in the pressures and excitement of the day – just as you do. I'd institute a firm schedule of a quiet rest period, say from 1 to 2 P.M. Firm, because he'll tease you to put it off. But if you know he needs it, as you do, you can make it stick. He doesn't have to sleep. But he needs to be by himself. Try reading to him or rocking him to quiet him down first. If he's having trouble sleeping at night, don't let him sleep after 3 P.M. Any sleep or rest after 4 P.M. can wreck the nighttime, for some reason.

QUESTION   I have a three-year-old and we have a hard time getting her down to bed at night. We have a steady routine and it's OK until we close the door; then she starts screaming and carrying on.

DR. BRAZELTON   She may sense that you are torn about leaving her. Some three-year-olds play on your emotions, saying, "I can't stand the door closed." When you leave it a crack open, they scream louder. They call out, "You don't love me," or "I'm afraid," or "I'm lonely, you have Daddy," or "Don't leave me!" Three-year-olds can be very resourceful, but you and your husband need and deserve time together, so settle your indecision! When she knows you have decided and you won't give in, she'll settle down more quickly. If she's had a family get-together, a play with Dad and a rock with Mom before going to bed, there's no reason for you to feel ambivalent. What she's doing is testing the limits of your indecision. You have to admire her determination, but you don't have to help her perpetuate it. After a while, let whichever one of you is the least ambivalent go in to tell her to be quiet and start getting herself to sleep. She'll act wounded, but she'll be relieved.

QUESTION

Our son is six months old and is having trouble sleeping. We're supplementing breast milk with solids. Should this help?

DR. BRAZELTON

Perhaps, but I've never been sure that hunger is a problem in the middle of the night. Parents blame hunger, a need for a food supplement, or teething – all sorts of other possible reasons – for night waking. I'm convinced that children learn to sleep through when we push them to learn how. A breast-feeding mother often feels that her baby isn't getting enough. If the baby is gaining weight, this is unlikely. It's possible that solids may help by lasting longer in the stomachs than milk alone. There is little evidence, but six months is a good time to start them anyway. You have to push him to sleep on his own a bit, too.

The Mazza Family Revisited

Since Linda worked every day, I was unable to see her except in the evening. I drove out to her house at eight o'clock one night. Linda lives well outside of Boston, close to other families and friends, near open countryside. Her small house was neat and trim. When I arrived, Linda and Andrew stood in the door, while Christopher came out to meet me. I was struck by how alike Linda and Andrew were, both in appearance and in gestures. Christopher must be like his father, for he is entirely different.

Now nine years old, Christopher is a tall, handsome, blond boy, clearly an athlete. He strutted around the house with his shirt off as if to demonstrate his already muscled torso. As he paced around, teasing his mother, he watched me for approval in very much the same direct, appealing way that I had noted in Linda. His manners were impeccable. As I arrived, he stuck out his hand, saying, "I've been wanting to see you." His whole aspect and demeanor belied his age of nine. I'd have placed him as an early adolescent on all counts. "He feels he needs to be the man of the family," said Linda. "He's never sure whether a new person will approve of him. He had a bad time with his father when he was little, and he's never been sure of himself since. Now he and his father have a good relationship, but the memory lingers on. Our divorce really shook him. He may still blame himself for it." Linda's concern for this boy's need to win approval reflects her own feelings as well. She is conscious of her son's precocious development, as well as the costs.

Andrew, now six and in first grade, is also tall and slender. His soft brown eyes take in the world around him, watching everything. He moves very little, and reacts to social overtures with slow, guarded responses. He, too, seemed to be watching to size me up when I entered the house. But in his case, I didn't get the same feeling, that of being looked to for approval. Instead, I felt he was trying to decide whether he approved of me. It made me overreact with a hearty, "Hi, Andrew, remember me?" Linda sensitively said, "Andrew, you remember Dr. Brazelton. You liked him so much!" – as if trying to nudge him into liking me again. Andrew smiled dutifully, but I didn't feel I'd gained any ground. If I looked back into those big eyes, he dropped his gaze to the floor, as if to say, "On my time – not yours!" It made me respect him as a person, but also wonder what feelings he was guarding. Again, Linda stepped in to help us out, saying, "Andrew takes his time with people. But when he likes you, he'll let you know it. He already knows how important you are to me."

I asked Linda what she meant.

"Well, you act as if you really care about what we went through. You listen. You don't just tell me what to do. The boys and I know when someone cares and when they don't. Having been through all the bad times we have had has taught us how to tell people from each other. We know who matters to us and who doesn't!"

She wanted to talk to me about where they were now, and, since that was just what I wanted to hear, we sat down at the kitchen table. Situated on the crest of a hill overlooking her in-laws' farmland, her neat little house seemed made for newlyweds. Linda said, "My life is so much better now." She sighed, "After six years, we are OK at last."

"Just OK?"

"Yes, just OK. But that's better than before. It's been a long, hard time. But it finally feels good. No one to disapprove of us. No one to interfere with our little trio. Even the boys say now, 'Mom, it's good this way – just us three.' I feel like we've made it."

"When we first met, it must have been in the midst of your recovery."

"We'd just begun to pull ourselves together. We hadn't begun to feel good about ourselves. Letting you see us as we were then was very, very hard. But you seemed to really understand what we were going through and to approve of how we were doing it. That meant an enormous amount to me."

I said I couldn't believe that our meetings could have been that helpful unless she was ready for the help they gave her. She smiled gratefully, and said, "That's what I mean. You turn what I say into self-respect for me. Everything I said to you at that time could have made me hurt. It could so easily have exposed my deep wounds. Instead you made me feel stronger for being able to expose myself. You made me feel healthy again."

I pointed out to her that I saw a person's ability to open herself and be honest about her children as a sign of strength. It was easy to see that this same strength was now paying off in the adjustment she'd made to a bad situation.

"Since we talked," said Linda, "I've met a man who is kind, who values me as a person — and I'm coming back together. But my boys still come first."

"All the way through it has sounded as if your boys came first, your other life second."

"Well, that's true. It might have been otherwise if I'd had a good marriage. But in this case, I'm lucky to have them to keep me together and sane."

"How will you let them go when you need to?"

"I don't know. I've thought a lot about that. What helped me was to start being aware that they were strong people in their own right. You see, when our marriage fell apart, I felt they were hurt, too. I felt as though I'd damaged them. You helped me see that I was hovering over Andrew because I felt I'd hurt him, and wanted him to be whole again. When you pointed out my overprotection and how competent he was as a four-year-old, I could begin to see him as a separate person. I began to let him take over. I could see he was able to manage by himself. It came as a huge surprise. He began to lead me. As I watched him and saw him handle himself in nursery school, and now in first grade, I began to feel whole again myself. I could see that he was popular, he was smart. He was good and kind. He's a leader in his class. Isn't that living proof?"

I commented that she'd been able to build a lot on just a few insights from me. She must have gotten her strength to follow through from somewhere. Was her family a help?

"Not too much. My sister felt my hurt too much and couldn't help me. My father wasn't that close anyway. Since my divorce, he has remarried, a divorced woman with children — so she understood my struggles. That helped. My neighbors here and my colleagues at work have been the real support. At the local hospital where I work, everyone knows what I've been through. I find it easy to talk to them. They've been a real help. They even saw to it that I met my present friend. Work has been my salvation. I can support my kids. I feel respect at work, which helps me as a parent.

"My boys have come a long way, too. From a daydreaming failure in school, Christopher is now a leader. He's up for a state leadership award; he's at the top of his class. He's an athlete and on every team."

I commented that Christopher certainly appeared to have made a real adjustment after his initial bad time. I asked Linda whether she worried about his being so good now, such a star. Was he ever negative or aggressive? At first she assured me that he was, but then she sat back in her chair, grew thoughtful and said, "Maybe I make him be too good. I'm like that, too. I grew up afraid of aggression. I never had to face it – until my marriage fell apart. When my husband became aggressive, I became more and more passive. It drove him crazy, I think. No marriage breaks up except with fifty-fifty blame. My trouble was that I couldn't be anything but 'good.' Now when Christopher begins to be aggressive or assertive, I pull away and look sad. He says, 'Mom, are you still there?' I think it frightens him when I withdraw. He's so afraid I won't be here."

"Does his aggression remind you of his father's?" She gave me one of the wide-eyed, amazed looks that I had seen before. "That's it. I am really afraid of him when he gets angry. It's not fair to him, is it? My husband used to say that, too. I don't want Chris to keep all his feelings inside of him. But I realize I've been asking him to be good for fear of the alternative."

She began to think about the way she treated Andrew as a baby. "I made him too good, too. I couldn't let him show any anger, any upset. I hovered over him for fear I'd have to discipline him. He had those sleeping problems, those fears of other children. All because I was afraid I couldn't be a disciplinarian. If he got out of hand, what would I do? Until you showed me that they *needed* limits. I began to let them try me out, to tease me. Now they know when I mean it, and when it's OK to push on me. We really understand each other. I always thought it would be hard to be a single parent – having to love and be a disciplinarian all in one. It's not. It's a very clear distinction. And no one's there to cloud it up. It's peaceful now."

As I looked at this deeply passionate young woman, I could see that she needed peace in which to nurture her boys. The peace which had eventually resulted from her divorce had been as critical to her as the chance to restore her own self-image. She was telling me why her marriage hadn't worked after the boys came. She needed a peaceful atmosphere for her sensitivity and style of mothering to blossom. With a critical, volatile husband, all of her assets disintegrated.

Her new friend, David, has been a real help in these past few years. He makes Linda feel worthwhile. He assures her that she's smart, pretty, and worthwhile. He protects her from any leftover feelings about her ex-husband. He cares about and respects the boys, and they love him. He takes them skiing, plays ball with them, wrestles with them. She can even let them be aggressive with David, but she can't let him discipline them. Would she marry again? "Not until the boys are bigger. Andrew says, 'I wish you'd marry Daddy.' And yet he never even knew him when we were married. Maybe that's why he wants me to get back into it. Daddy, to him, is someone who gives him presents on the weekends. Christopher would never want that. He saw his father beat me up and he's afraid of that. Christopher says, 'It's OK just the three of us.' After David has been here, Christopher talks like him. He even teases me like David does: 'You're getting old,' or 'You're getting chunky.' He probably needs a father so he can quit having to be one."

"What would you want other divorcing parents to know?"

"That it takes a while before you begin to feel like a human being again," said Linda. "You are bound to feel degraded, and a failure. But after a while all of it begins to come back. I feel more together, more at peace now than I did before my divorce. I wouldn't recommend divorce to my worst enemy, but if it is necessary, I'd tell someone that she can and will make it."

I told her that Judith Wallerstein's research showed that it took children about five years before they really recovered from the effects of divorce. They never stopped longing for a reconciliation between their parents, but they adjusted, and by five years they demonstrated no residual behavioral effects.

Linda brightened and said, "That's it. It does take that long, but what you need during those years is to realize that you will make it eventually. While it was going on, I realized that my grieving was affecting them, so I tried reading to them about other families who were 'like us.' I wish we'd had a group of other families in the same situation to turn to. For the first two years, I told them how to think. That was no good. As soon as I began to let them do their own thinking, their own deciding, they felt better. I hovered, for fear they'd be scarred. Instead, my hovering made them feel scarred. As soon as I let go, they snapped to and have been real people ever since. When you worry about being a single parent, you take every developmental step too seriously. I'd advise all parents what you advised me: 'Give them room and trust them to do it themselves. You can help children get through a bad time but you can't do it for them.' They know what you are going through and they don't need to have it repeated over and over. They worry about the same things you do. By trying to protect them, you give them a subtle message, that they are weak and helpless. Now, I share things openly with them. We talk it out with each other and we come to a mutual agreement on how we'll do it as a family. Never having enough money has been the hardest for them to understand. But now they say, 'Mom, can we afford this? If not, can we all save up for it?' They feel as good as I do that I can make it for them on my job. We all pitch in and it works for us."

As I listened to her, with the boys nearby, I realized that her respect for them allowed her to share her concerns openly. I pointed out that she was giving these boys a very precious experience – a feeling of truly sharing in the family's survival. This kind of responsible caring for one another was rare in our society. "Yes," Linda said, "each of us has chores in making our life work. But I do worry that they're having to grow up too early." I pointed out that there were positive aspects to this kind of growing up. Not enough children in our affluent society really have to pitch in to make a house work. Not many children can look back on the sense of shared trust and the bonds of overcoming a crisis that Linda had given them. I did worry about Christopher's feeling that he had to be a successful surrogate father for Andrew, and also that he had to be so good at hiding his aggression, but I felt Linda had heard me as we discussed these issues. She had an ability to take a question in and pick up on it later.

I asked her whether she ever got away from them. "Two long weekends in six years," she said. "I left them with their grandparents, my in-laws. They are good to them. Their father takes them for one night but never two. He has his own limits, I guess. But I'm not sure I want him to take them for too long."

"Are you afraid they'll like him better if he does, and end up deserting you?"

"Yes, of course. He used to tease me by saying he'd take them away someday. It scared me to death. Now I see that he really can't handle them for too long, so I know he wouldn't. It's a real relief. But he just indulges them, never disciplines them. I'm always the bad guy. Will they turn to him later? I don't want them to go to him or to be like him as teenagers. How do I avoid this?" Again, this came as a rather childlike appeal. "When they rebel, they say, 'I'm going to live with Daddy for a while!' It terrifies me." I assured her that the relationship seemed too good for that to me. But this fear did contribute to a different kind of hovering, a kind of wooing them to stay close to her. It made it hard for them ever to let go of her. Did she want that?

Her eyes clouded over as she responded, "Oh Lord, underneath I know I'm going to ruin them some way or other. I feel I must make up to them for being a single parent, for being hurt by a divorce. When things are going well, I have a feeling of doom. I can't help but feel that sooner or later we will crash again. Will I be strong enough? When they're teenagers, can I take it? Can I keep their respect? See, I keep on being afraid that I haven't given them the right start."

I pointed out that fear could be more damaging than any reality. Not only are about half the children in our present generation facing this kind of family disruption, but Linda's awareness of their needs, and her ability to use this sensitivity to help them face their own adjustments, were enormous assets for their future.

The Mazza Family Revisited

Her eyes glowed again; her whole face became grateful as I offered support for her valiant efforts.

"One thing I've learned," she said, is "that strength without gentleness isn't real strength. I wanted Christopher and Andrew to be strong in the right way." She smiled. "Well, as you can see, I'll always find something new to worry about! The hardest but most important job seems to be to learn when and how to let a child go. To do this, I had to grow up myself."

As we finished our visit, I felt a deep respect for Linda's struggle. She had confronted the problem of simple parenthood successfully. Though her sense of impending doom still called for work on her part, she is not a depressed person any longer. Two short years ago, she had seemed very sad. At that time, her anxiety was fostering sleep and separation problems in Andrew. With the very little help and insight gained from our meetings, she was able to open herself up to a real self-evaluation. She was a very good listener, aware enough of her own needs to be able to separate her problems from those of the boys. As soon as she did this, Andrew settled down and went off to his nursery school with a sense of independence. Both boys grew up "before my eyes." She, in turn, gathered strength from them. She solidified a relationship with David and began to give Christopher and Andrew more space. Each of the boys is now manly, secure, caring, and responsible. They are a great team and can be proud of one another and of themselves.

The Considine
Family

‌ઽ

CHAPTER III

The Considine Family

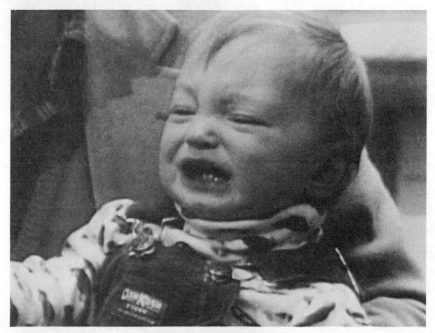

The Considine Family

Family History

Tommy, who is sixteen months old, is the third child in what I can only describe as a picture-book family. His sisters – Sarah, five, and Becky, three – have big blue eyes, wavy blond hair, and winsome, round faces. When they both look up at you at the same time, it's a Victorian album come to life. Sarah and Becky are gentle, polite, well-mannered, and eager to please adults and visitors as well as their family. They are particularly conscious of Tom, their father. Tom was one of eleven children in a New England Catholic family. At thirty-four, he is already a brilliantly successful executive in a small computer programming business. As a graduate student he studied child development and anthropology. He then began the computer business with one of his brothers. He met Susan, an artist, in college. She is from a smaller, perhaps less ambitious, family of three children from the Middle West. Before leaving work to have Sarah, she designed toys and illustrated children's books. Tom's business takes him away from the family more than they had planned.

Both Susan and Tom love children and have admitted to themselves that, had they married earlier, they probably would have had more than three. Both wanted a boy, but among their social set in Cambridge, Massachusetts, it is not acceptable to admit to preferring one sex over the other. Girls and boys are to be thought of as equals and of equal value in a family. Although they lavish affection on all three, I noticed that they both treat Tommy with a shade more reverence. He gets just a bit more attention.

Sarah and Becky are more subdued now since Tommy was born. They tiptoe about quietly, as if on egg shells. Their parents expect them to show good manners, and believe that only civilized behavior will ensure that others enjoy their company and that they will enjoy each other's. Indeed, everyone around them does gasp with delight at these two lovely, outgoing girls. They seem to know how to please the adults around them. They do it without strain,

The Considine Family

in an easy manner. They are close, and so they turn to one another for restraint when it is necessary. They blow up, of course, as any normal child would do, but only occasionally, and so I wonder if their habit of pleasing everybody so consistently isn't proving to be too costly to them emotionally. I wonder how much of it is their reaction to being displaced by the baby. Many children who are "good" on the surface take it out on themselves. They show the strain of always pleasing adults in their worried and tense expressions. Others show symptoms of stress whenever the pressures around them increase, as well as when adults are not showing constant, open approval. Sarah and Becky take out their tensions on each other, sharing them, and display subtly competitive behaviors. They use their closeness to maintain balance and as a way of mirroring each other's social graces. They are an appealing twosome.

Susan came to see me for a prenatal visit during her first pregnancy. Her main concern was the activity of the fetus, which bounced around and kept Susan awake from 2 to 5:30 in the morning, and again from 4 to 6 P.M. We predicted then that she might be active, especially at those times of the day, after she was born. She was. She cried half the day and developed colic. Her mother carried her a lot, constantly trying out different maneuvers to quiet her, but the more she hovered, the more Sarah cried. In fact, she kept it up four to five hours a day, mercilessly, waking every two to three hours at night. This exhausted Susan, who decided to wean Sarah from the breast at four months.

In my office, Tom, Susan, and I repeatedly discussed the causes of the crying. It was my opinion that a baby should be left to overcome some of it herself. Once Susan had tried everything she knew to calm Sarah, I recommended that she let her fuss for ten minutes at a time before she comforted her. In that way, she'd "let off steam" and get her need to cry over with in a regular, contained fussy period every day. Susan could not do that. She was unable to take any solace from the fact that a certain amount of crying each day was a normal part of a baby's cycle of rest and activity. She told me how difficult it was for her to hear a baby cry. She felt that a baby's cry was a call for help, and that a mother should respond. Among her earliest memories was the sound of her own little sister crying. No one went to her, and Susan had resented her mother's coldness, and she felt guilty at her own inability to help her sister. Now she felt compelled to go to her own baby and to do everything she could to calm her. Even if it didn't work, she still couldn't bear to let the baby cry alone. By constantly trying, she felt that at least she was doing her job. After all, she asked, it didn't hurt the baby, did it?

As I listened, I realized that she'd have to do it her way, not mine. I developed a real respect for Susan and her determination. It has gotten her through other crises. And I've learned when to offer advice and when not to.

When Sarah was fourteen months old she righted herself and began to sleep through the night. She became docile and eager to please, and I've never entirely understood how this came about. She seemed to realize that she no longer needed to make the same demands she had been making. Somehow she sensed that her mother's responses to her were a way of nurturing her and that she had had enough of nurturing. Sarah is now a competent, easy, well-adjusted preschooler. She appears to have settled her inner struggles and now values her independence. She in turn nurtures Tommy, running to help him or comfort him or satisfy him in some way, very much like her mother did for her. And she is gentle and kind with Becky, in fact, an unusually even-tempered child. I would never have predicted it from her infancy. Susan and Tom's approach, that is, satisfying her every whim, seems to have worked. This kind of caring involvement in Sarah's welfare, which I didn't fully understand at the time, probably met an emotional need that Susan had (as she had so firmly stated). It certainly satisfied the driving intensity I saw in the baby Sarah.

Becky, also active *in utero*, was not an easy child in the beginning, either. She, too, cried continually with colic pain. Susan breast-fed her almost constantly and succeeded in containing her crying spells by the time Becky was three months old. By then, she was round and healthy, and heavy to carry. Throughout her first few years she continued to wake up, at least once, each night. As soon as she discovered that she could walk she would go to her exhausted mother's bed each night. This went on until Becky was two-and-a-half years old. Susan and Tom would let her stay. They

The Considine Family

tried not to cross her. Her strong temperament now dominated the family; Sarah had given way, and Becky was next in line, demanding the attention that Sarah had gotten before. Her parents thought of her as "difficult" and did not try to toilet-train her until she was two. At that point, she caught on to the idea and so trained herself, "almost overnight."

When they brought Tommy home from the hospital, Tom and Susan were surprised to discover that they had to focus on Becky, not the new baby. At first she was temperamental; she wouldn't speak, she ground her teeth at night, and her allergies to foods and pollens became more severe – all symptoms of the extent of the adjustment she was having to make to the new baby. This time I gave no advice to Susan and Tom. I respected the fact that they seemed to know exactly how they wanted to handle this period of transition. As I watched them all struggle through the first few months of Tommy's babyhood, I could see Becky begin to calm down, to become the organized, pleasing child she is now – almost a replica of her big sister. At times, she still seemed stormy, but always under control.

Tommy is not at all like his sisters. As a newborn he was calm, dogged, and determined, and he still is. None of the turmoil of his sisters' first years was evident in him. As is often the case, he is more like his mother, and the girls seem to be more like Tom – active, intense, dramatic – at least they were before they became more subdued. Now, who can tell? Is the behavior I see only "surface" behavior? Are they suppressing a tumultuous interior underneath?

Tommy has a congenital problem in the retina of one eye, which no one can explain. His vision is not seriously affected, but it is causing his parents a good deal of unspoken concern. Their perfect little boy must be accepted as not quite perfect – a difficult prospect for any parents. He has allergic skin rashes as well, and bronchitis. To avoid the eczema and asthma prevalent in his father's family, it was necessary to begin early to control his diet and the allergens in his environment. Susan and Tom worked hard at this, and now we all feel confident that we can keep his allergies under control. My approach to allergies is to advise patients to try to avoid all of the allergens, however mild, that together might combine to build up to a real challenge. If strong reactions to allergies can be avoided, by the normal process of maturation, a child's rising threshold of sensitivity will gradually solve the problem. Time and reduced exposure to allergens are factors on our side. So far, at fourteen months, Tommy has avoided a reaction, and so I consider that we have been successful.

Crying

&

OFFICE VISIT

As Susan, Tom, and I talked, the three children played in my waiting room. Tommy moved with determination to upset any buildings that his sisters had made with blocks. He was silent, but destructive, and his sisters never crossed him, nor even deterred him. I watched with amazement. When his sisters finally did block the way, Tommy cried loudly for help. I watched Susan jump to help him.

SUSAN
I'm just learning how to understand Tommy when he cries. He's very frustrated now, because he's falling down a lot, stumbling over things, and Sarah and Becky take things away from him. That cry is familiar; it's one of anger and frustration.

DR. BRAZELTON
Yes, you called me the other day about his crying, and I thought we might try to deal with it while you are here. Does he cry a lot at night as well?

SUSAN
He's crying now at night more than he used to, and he's also crying more during the day. It's a different kind of cry, though. I think I can tell all his different cries. He tries to talk but can't say much yet, so I have to go by his cries to figure out what he wants.

DR. BRAZELTON　　In what way is it different? *I'm always amazed how a parent is so attuned to every nuance of a baby's cry.*

SUSAN　　If he's frustrated, it is shriller and stops in a matter of seconds. If he's lonely, it is sadder, and he keeps it up until someone shows up.

DR. BRAZELTON　　What about his crying at night? Is that a problem?

TOM　　It seemed like it got worse briefly when he started getting teeth.

SUSAN　　Yes, it began with his teeth. Until that time, he would sleep seven hours, even eight or nine hours. But when he started teething, he started waking up. When I went in and said, "I'll hold you and give you something to drink," probably I reinforced this pattern. Now I'm trying to break him of it.

DR. BRAZELTON　　How do you do that?

SUSAN　　I don't run instantly when he cries, hoping that maybe he'll pull himself out of it, straighten himself out. That's working a little bit. Or else, I go in without picking him up, and simply reassure him that I'm there, pat him on the back, shake him just a bit, and then leave the room.

DR. BRAZELTON　　Good for you. One of the hardest things about parenting is the crying. In the beginning, it's particularly tough. Crying makes a huge demand on you. First of all, it stirs you up, and you feel, "I've got to do something about it."

The Considine Family

It causes a kind of alarm reaction in a parent that he or she can't ignore.

SUSAN   It took me a while. The third time around, I can handle it better. But recently . . .

DR. BRAZELTON Yes?

I sensed there was more.

SUSAN   He seems so frustrated. Tommy is the third, and sometimes I don't think I'm giving him enough attention. My time is so divided between these three, all with different needs. Sarah now can write her name perfectly. She can write her daddy's name, she can write everybody's name and loves to show it to me. I am really torn in all different ways. While Sarah's learning all this, I've got Becky working on ABCs, her reds and greens. And here's Tommy over here, wanting to get up and walk with me. At night, everyone's trying to learn to brush their teeth. It's a three-ring circus. How do I get out of this "get me a glass of water" business? I mean, I'm all over the place, frantic all the time. So it's hard for me to pay enough attention to Tommy, because I can't keep up with everybody.

Susan believes Tommy is crying out for attention, for the love a busy mother wants to give but can't. His cries touch a chord in her and make her feel how torn apart she is – having three kids and not enough time to go around.

SUSAN   I'm feeling guilty, because I don't think I'm giving him – I can't afford to give him – the same things Sarah had. Sarah had me one-to-one, and the others won't have me that way.

It's hard for me to juggle them, especially hard to pay attention when he cries.

DR. BRAZELTON He's taking it out on you. These cries are healthy, positive signs of normal development. But you were also telling me that he's just beginning to talk to you. He wants to communicate, not just to capture your attention, which is what he's up to now. That's a big step. In fact, he's ahead of himself in trying so hard to speak. He can't wait to get there even faster. Some of the crying may be sheer impatience. Tommy is crying out for his exciting new world! And you're the one he wants to talk to. Maybe you're taking his crying too seriously. It may be just a form of communication at a time when he can't speak in any other way.

THE ISSUES

A crying baby can change a well-ordered household into a disordered nightmare. An inconsolable baby will reduce even the most composed adult to a state of frenzied helplessness. Parents say they feel desperate when they can't comfort their crying baby. A caring adult instinctively knows that there must be a solution, and if he could only find it the infant would stop. When he can't, he feels like a failure and is reduced to frantic, useless attempts to quiet the crying infant. Often these simply increase the tension in an already wrought-up situation. They fuel the crying, rather than reduce it.

It helps to understand that crying for a small infant serves many purposes, not the least of which is as an outlet for his tension and pent-up energy. Crying shuts out disturbing stimuli which the infant can't handle otherwise. It is, like sleep, a barrier against stimulation. In each of these states of consciousness, he is relatively unavailable, so a parent's earnest efforts to quiet him may go awry.

The Considine Family

One new mother of a colicky baby showed me how she quieted him – by bouncing him vigorously up and down, throwing him high in the air after each bounce. Of course, he quieted temporarily – perhaps out of sheer terror – but he soon started crying again, even more lustily, after the bouncing stopped.

Over the years at Children's Hospital, we have shown in our research that normal babies at first cry for a period of one to one-and-a-half hours a day up to three weeks of age, then build up to two hours (some to four hours) by six weeks. As they begin to smile, to vocalize, and to become more organized in other kinds of social responses, the crying starts to decrease, and it pretty much dies out by twelve weeks. This fussy period is predictably at the end of the day for most families, and in all cases, when vigorous efforts are made to keep the baby quiet, the crying increases. When parents are able to allow their baby to work out his own solution, the fussy periods diminish.

There are also some marked individual differences among babies. The ones who suck a great deal don't seem to need to cry very much. The quiet, watchful ones who sleep a lot almost seem to choose sleep over fussing – as some sort of trade-off. Sometimes in noisy households, a new baby will quietly sleep all day, only to cry at night when the household is quiet. Riding in the car, or turning on the radio or television, or any other continuous noise, does seem to quiet some babies – temporarily at least. When there are too many people – grandparents, father, a nurse – who criticize the mother, blame her for her lack of milk, say, or for some inadequacy in dealing with the baby, one can predict that the baby will cry more and be less easily quieted. Anxiety in the household always increases crying – but it doesn't account for it in the first place.

My advice to parents on how to handle crying is based on my observation that most babies need a time to let off steam, to discharge all of the tension they have stored up during the day. I urge new parents to try first all the tricks they know to quiet the baby: feed, change, rock, hold, cuddle, use swaddling or a pacifier, and so on – but when all of these no longer work, let the baby handle it. And he will. If parents leave him to fuss or cry for twenty minutes at a time, then pick him up, calm him down, give him

Crying

some sugar water to help get up the air he's gulped, then put him down to cry for another twenty-minute period, it gets all the crying over with in an expectable evening period. And the rest of his day and night are likely to be better organized thereafter.

In a classic study Drs. Bell and Ainsworth at Johns Hopkins followed a group of infants whose mothers responded to their crying after varying periods of delay before comforting them. They found that the group of babies whose mothers came right away to pick them up and soothe them, and who then went on about their own business, cried less when they were a year old. The infants who were allowed to cry for a while (fifteen to twenty minutes) *before* their mothers came to find out why they were crying were likely to be "crybabies" still at a year old. In other words, responding to a baby quickly does not necessarily reinforce his crying for attention, and suggests that a parent's role may best be served by going to the baby *soon after* he started crying, trying to find out if anything needs to be done, and instituting a barrage of soothing maneuvers. Then, if the maneuvers no longer work, leave the baby alone to handle it for himself.

In several studies, researchers have tried to tape the various cries of an infant, and to diagnose – from analysis of the tapes, and from any known stimulus – what each cry meant. For example, cries can mean hunger, pain, wet, mad, "pick me up," or just "leave me alone." Crying is a rich language for a baby. Dr. Barry Lester, a psychologist and researcher in infant behavior, has studied crying and cries by means of a spectrographic technique, and has demonstrated the differences between pain, hunger, boredom, anger, the cry of waking up or going to sleep, and the cry of a baby who is overloaded at the end of the day. All of these cries show a distinct pattern on the spectrograph. Dr. Lester also investigated how long it takes new parents to tell these differences. They begin to differentiate them by the time the infant is ten days old, and by the time he is three to four weeks of age they can usually tell if it's pain or boredom or hunger. The cry that is hardest for them to differentiate, but that is very different on tape, is the cry of "colic" at the end of the day. It does not look at all like real pain. Dr. Lester's research shows that a pain cry begins as a long wail, then a long period of breathholding, then a short breath and rest, followed by another wail, then a period of breathholding. This rhythm goes on until the baby is exhausted. Colic looks very different. It has a short burst, then tapering off, then a short breath, then another crescendo, with a long tailing off.

As a child gets older, his cries become easier to differentiate. They become intentional signals, and the intention becomes clearer to those around him. A painful cry retains its piercing character and can be differentiated from other cries, because it continues even when the baby is picked up. Cries of frustration or anger can be differentiated more easily. A cry of "pick me up" or of "leave me alone" is accompanied by clear gestures.

In toddlers, there are at least three kinds of crying a parent needs to be aware of. They come in the second year, and as a surprise to most parents. The first is a cry of frustration and anger when a child has trouble mastering a project. In particular, at each new surge of learning – crawling, sitting up, standing, walking – a baby's awareness of the new ability, and his desire to get there, may outstrip his capacity to achieve the new, foreseen step. The unbalance sets up a kind of inner frustration which makes him cry with anger at himself. This frustration to achieve can become a powerful motivating force. However, if parents misinterpret these cries of frustration as cries for help, and rush in, the child's need to achieve becomes overwhelmed and diffused. Instead of being encouraged to keep trying, the child is rewarded for his whimpering dependency.

In the second year, as a child begins to experience autonomy and the excitement it brings him, he may also begin to sense a need for limits. He may even begin to tease his parents to set limits. By provoking his parents into action, he learns when to stop himself. This dawning awareness of the need for limits is amazing to me. A child will deliberately set up a situation in which parents must respond with firmness; when they don't, his disappointment is reflected by increased negative, provocative behavior. The child may even begin to fall apart; crying, he almost *demands* that they end his teasing episode. When his parents do not respond with firmness, his anxiety mounts, as does his "spoiled" behavior. The feeling that the onlooker has, of wanting to stop him, to contain him, is a kind of intuition about just what he is calling for by his behavior. A "spoiled" child is an anxious child. He seeks the firmness of an assured parent.

A third kind of crying comes with the disintegration represented by temper tantrums in the early part of the second year. Parents call me about their toddler's first temper tantrum, wondering what they've done wrong, and asking me how they can stop it. I think temper tantrums, and the cries of helpless anger that accompany them in the second year, are likely to be a normal step in a vital, outgoing toddler's development. When he reaches the stage of determination, as he learns to walk and to achieve a kind of mastery over his environment, he will be caught up in his desire to become independent and to achieve *on his own*. But he may not be very sure of himself yet. He has to decide between, "Yes, I want to" and "No, I don't think I can." He has to make decisions which are important to him but which may not seem very important to those around him. As he tries desperately to decide, he is likely to disintegrate into a crying, blubbering heap – consumed by a temper tantrum. Parents may feel they should help, or should contain or stop these outbursts. As they try, the episode increases, and that is the signal that it's the child's own struggle. As a parent, you can be of very little help at the time, but you can comfort him later for the depth of his struggle. At the time, any effort from you just fuels his tortured misery. It is very hard for parents to see that tantrums are not cries for help, but represent an inner struggle, with powerful, ambivalent forces at work, which is important to the child's development.

Crying is a window into the child's developing strengths. I am always relieved to see a vital child express himself clearly. I would rather see a child cry out loud in protest, or in anger or frustration, than to feel that he must bury it deep inside, to deal with it alone. Although it may be hard for the parent to witness, a crying child is expressing healthy feelings. The parent's task is to learn when it's a cry for help and when it must be handled by the child.

In my office, toddlers cry about my invading their personal space. They are protecting their body from the assaults of a stranger, and I try to respect their new awareness of the necessity to do so. If I acknowledge their anxiety as appropriate by first examining a doll and then their parent, they allow me to examine them without protest. One could easily misinterpret this crying as fear, but it seems more like a need for respect.

COMMON QUESTIONS

QUESTION   What is colic? My baby, at the end of the day, won't stop crying hysterically.

DR. BRAZELTON   Colic represents the discharge of an already overloaded, immature, and raw central nervous system. It can receive and respond to stimuli all day, but it builds up a little bit of overload each time. Finally, at the end of the day, it blows. The baby seems to "need" to let off steam in order to get ready for the next twenty-four hours. There are only a few ways to get reorganized if you are immature – either by sleeping, by being very active, or by crying. The fact that this kind of cry is so hard to stop by any of the normal parenting maneuvers probably means that it may be serving an important purpose for the baby.

QUESTION   When I come home from work at the end of the day, my baby takes one look at me and starts crying. What causes that?

DR. BRAZELTON   I'm afraid you're just one more set of exciting stimuli at the end of a long day. Also, your baby may pick up the excitement in the household that you cause, and he certainly senses how eager you are to see him. It's hard not to take it personally, isn't it? After this period is over, he'll be great again. Try to wait it out. He needs you to get close to him.

Crying

QUESTION   Why does colic end at three months?

DR. BRAZELTON   By three months, the baby's maturing nervous system can handle stimuli better. She can smile, vocalize, and communicate in other, more effective ways. If colicky crying goes on longer, there may be other reasons for it, such as milk or hypersensitivity. By then, I'd get help with it. Consult your doctor. One baby I had in my practice cried because her mother was unreachable. She was trying to warn us that her mother was depressed.

QUESTION   How can you tell whether crying means something serious or not?

DR. BRAZELTON   In a young baby, when crying is regular at the end of each day, when it stops temporarily as you pick the baby up, but starts in again as you put him down, it's not likely to be anything you need to feel too concerned about, especially if the baby is gaining weight and doing well in other ways. Try picking him up, giving him something to suck, changing his diapers, rocking and holding him. If these work, you've found the answer. If they don't work at all and the baby continues to build up to more crying, you do have to worry about pain. Then press on him all around to see whether you can localize the pain. Even press down on his belly. Fortunately, a baby in pain will let you know when you've hit a sore spot. He will let out a real cry of pain. Small children are usually not hard to read at all. If the crying goes on for an unusual length of time and you have not located the cause, call the doctor.

The Considine Family

QUESTION

My little girl uses crying to manipulate all of us. When she wants her way, she just lies down on the floor to cry, looking us straight in the face, as if to say, "Do what I tell you – or else." Is she already spoiled?

DR. BRAZELTON

I never quite know what "being spoiled" means. It is probably different for each person. My own concept of a spoiled child is one who is asking for firm limits. When she doesn't get them, she may become somewhat anxious, wondering when the axe will fall. In your little girl's case, I would bet that she's indeed trying you all out. She's feeling her independence and wants to test the limits of what she can do to manipulate all of you. If you want her crying to stop, I'd suggest that you stop reinforcing it in any way. When you know she's not in trouble or in pain, just walk away from her. Afterward, pick her up to hug her and say, "I don't like it when you cry that way. I love you, and I want to hug you, so just tell me when you need something, but don't cry about it." Either a positive or a negative response at the time of the outburst will reinforce it. It is pretty common for a strong-minded two-year-old to use crying to get what she wants.

Middle Child

ઐ

HOUSE CALL

When I arrived at the Considines' house, Sarah and Becky greeted me at the door, their pretty, fresh faces aglow.

DR. BRAZELTON Hi, girls. How are you?

The girls smiled eagerly. They were proud to show me their house.

SUSAN Becky's doing much better now. Her temperature's gone.

DR. BRAZELTON I'm glad to hear that.

SUSAN But she's been waking up more during the night and having restless sleep. Sometimes it's a dream, and you can hear her say something very clearly. We weren't sure when we first heard her whether it was due to her allergies or to the repercussions of the flu.

DR. BRAZELTON She's waking up every night?

SUSAN Most nights.

DR. BRAZELTON And what else? *To Becky.* Have you been feeling awful?

She didn't look ill, but something's been brewing with Becky. It all started last year. Sarah was playing the big sister to the hilt,

The Considine Family

always a step ahead of Becky. And Tommy, the baby of the family, was about to take his first steps. In the middle was Becky; calm on the surface, but beneath it, highly sensitive and moody. Too much so. Tom and Susan thought it was allergies.

TOM   It got so that every single morning she'd wake up screaming. We decided that maybe she had an allergy to something; we didn't know what it was. So we started giving her antihistamines on a steady twenty-four-hour dosage, and after four days, she started waking up smiling. Instead of screaming, she'd wake up and say, "Hi, I did get up by myself."

SUSAN   There's been a big improvement here; it's like a whole new child.

Their treatment, well-meaning, may have worked for a while, but blaming this behavior on allergies was too simple for a complex child like Becky.

DR. BRAZELTON   What else has changed?

SUSAN   She's more on her own now, because Sarah's gone off to school.

DR. BRAZELTON   This is really her first time without Sarah, isn't it?

SUSAN   That's right.

DR. BRAZELTON   The first time in her life without Sarah!

SUSAN   She looked to Sarah for a lot of guidance.

DR. BRAZELTON   It takes a lot of courage to get up every day all by yourself, doesn't it, Becky?

Middle Child

Becky was probably upset. Still, I wanted to examine her. I had to make sure.

SUSAN   She said this morning that her tummy didn't sleep last night.

DR. BRAZELTON   Oh dear, Becky. Let's listen to you, can we? Can you take your dress off for a minute? Let me check you.

A lot of middle children hold their feelings in. Illness might be Becky's way of letting those feelings out. I'm trying to size up whether it's physical or whether there's something else going on.

DR. BRAZELTON   You do look a little bit pale. Let's check your tummy. Mommy says sometimes your tummy bothers you. Does it bother you right now? You know, I think you look very good. Your stomach's OK, and your throat's OK. Maybe Mommy and I could talk about you a little bit. Could you and Sarah go out in the kitchen and play? *To Susan.* Well, I think she's physically all right, but I think she may be worried about what's going on this year. You know, Sarah's really dominated her life, and to be separated is really quite a shock. The trouble with Becky is that she doesn't express anything directly. She shoves it all under, and you don't know 'til later what's been bothering her. Maybe it's what we call "the middle-child syndrome." Her stomachaches, her need to have you come and comfort her every night all over again, suggest this. Remember how she needed the same reassurance two and a half years ago before Tommy came?

SUSAN   She seems to want help with everything. When she needs to be corrected, whereas I say to

The Considine Family

Sarah, "Pick up your room," and Sarah will do it, I say, "Becky . . ." and Becky will say, "I don't know how to do that." I have to help her, as though she were a baby again.

DR. BRAZELTON   So you think this is a kind of regression, back to being a baby?

SUSAN   I think she feels cheated and needing attention. She wants much more physical contact with me.

DR. BRAZELTON   You know, she really is squeezed right in the middle. She's got that stubborn, cunning little boy who's suddenly gotten into everything and is driving everybody up the wall but having a fabulous time at it. Everybody loves him, because he's so glorious. Then, there's Sarah on top, going to school, to a big school. I know no one is ignoring Becky. But she may wonder: what's left for Becky?

SUSAN   Sometimes I feel sorry for her. I know that's wrong, and I shouldn't feel that way because that's not helping her or helping me help her. But I feel bad for her sometimes.

DR. BRAZELTON   Why?

SUSAN   Because I don't know how to help her feel comfortable with herself.

DR. BRAZELTON   But do you need to do it for her? She may be able to manage for herself.

SUSAN   Well, I didn't feel she could, I guess.

Middle Child

There was little Susan could do. Making it too smoothed over was not really helping right now.

DR. BRAZELTON   It is painful to think about, isn't it?

SUSAN   Yes. Poor Becky. You know, I was a middle child and felt deserted when the baby came. Here it is all over again.

Here's the crux. Susan feels identified with her.

DR. BRAZELTON   She's a strong girl. Look what she's achieved already. But I've got to warn you about one thing. The more independent she gets and the more open she gets about her feelings, the more she's going to push Sarah away from her. She's going to make Sarah desert her. Sarah's going to turn to Tommy. That's going to be the hardest thing of all, because they have been so close. For a while, she may feel really alone. She may need to regress and ask for help in order to gather steam.

SUSAN   She'll be like an island out there. It's scary.

DR. BRAZELTON   That's the next hardest thing about being a middle child. Being deserted by your mother for the baby may be the hardest, but the second trial is to relive it through your older sister or brother leaving you, too.

SUSAN   I always feel that she's in this glass bubble, and if I put her down or let her alone, she's

The Considine Family

going to break. She seems more vulnerable than Sarah.

DR. BRAZELTON Some of this is for your benefit. If you look at her carefully, she's making it. Hovering over her or identifying with the fact that she's a middle child and feels so sorry for herself isn't going to make her stronger. I don't think she's as vulnerable as she looks. I'm not worried about her. Make sure your worries are not memories of your own problems as a child. When you identify too much with her, you may reinforce her feeling of being inadequate, when she's really not.

Becky came back into the room, and Susan looked at her. She can see for herself – Becky standing there on her own two feet, holding her own.

THE ISSUES

How does a label get started? When does a second child begin to feel like a "middle child"? Why does this label stick to a middle child all through her life?

The first child always holds a special place. Parents shower the first child, not only with all of their special attention, but also with their special anxieties. The first child is the experimental child. New parents must try themselves out with a first child, succeeding and failing, learning as they go along. As a result, every new step in this child's development seems to be partly theirs. Nothing the child ever does is divorced from the parents' sense of intense investment.

The second child comes and is likely to be very different from the first child. Many second children are openly competitive and are perfectionists. Many are quietly determined to live up to the first child – prizing his or her qualities just as the parents do. The second child is set up to take a secondary role, but fights against it with strong competitive feelings. These feelings hide a deeper conviction that she will "never really make it." When parents sense this, they are likely to try to reassure a second child, to overcompensate in an attempt to destroy the myth. But their efforts may serve only to confirm her conviction, since they themselves know the real truth – that she'll always be "second."

When a third child comes, the competition is disrupted, and parents are likely to sigh with relief. Now, the second child won't have to feel like she's on the bottom, so they turn their attention to the third baby. Their experience has given them assurance and expertise; number three seems like a real cinch. Usually, the third child is like a "dividend" and quickly takes a special place in the eyes and hearts of the parents. At first, the oldest child expects a repetition of the anguish and anger felt when the first sibling, the middle child, was born. But this new baby is different. This time the new baby's "babyishness" is appealing. The oldest child "deserts" the second sibling in favor of the new one. Now everyone's attention is centered on the third child, and the middle child syndrome is set. Middle children must compete with both an older and a younger sibling. If they try to beat out number one, they are likely to fail. If they try to identify with the baby, everyone is scornful and reproving. "Don't act like a baby!" What is cute in a baby is scolded in the middle child. In school, middle children are reminded of what their older sibling achieved. Middle children feel as though they have no place to turn.

When parents empathize with this, they may quietly reinforce it, unless they face their own feelings. It becomes critical that parents think very carefully about individual differences. Value the special characteristics of each child, but without too much emphasis. Too much praise rings hollow. Don't overreact. Give the second child a special time with each parent, as you give each of the others. Don't use that time for anyone else. Talk about it all week so that she knows it's coming, can anticipate it, and decide what you will do together. Use it as a time to get to know the middle child as a special person. If she needs it, take another child of her same age along, to help her develop a friendship. If you get to know the "middle child" as a special person, you will both soon forget the label, and the special relationship you develop with her will be more important to her than her place in the line-up.

COMMON QUESTIONS

QUESTION   My middle child tries to get attention by fighting with his older and younger brothers. How can I handle this?

DR. BRAZELTON   First of all, stay out of their fights as much as you can. Let them learn about each other without your being the focus of their attention. He may be trying to identify with either the "big boy" or the "baby" to get your praise and attention. When you are alone with him, point out that he has special qualities all his own. Help him feel that he doesn't need to be like them.

QUESTION   Can you avoid the middle child syndrome by having more than three children?

DR. BRAZELTON   Having a big family won't avoid the middle-child syndrome. If you feel torn, you may create many "middle children." The fact is, these feelings are in the child's mind and yours, not in the situation. I'm not sure you can ever avoid them completely. A child who picks up your feelings of being pulled in too many directions will label herself no matter what. The best you can do is not to be trapped by the label. "Look," you can say, "you're just as special as Amy or Thalia. You've just got to believe in yourself. I can't do that for you." Having more and more babies won't help.

Middle Child

QUESTION   Are there studies and statistics on how children do, depending on where they come in
the family?

DR. BRAZELTON   Yes, there are. They conclude that there are
more presidents and eminently successful peo-
ple who are first children. What they neglect
to point out is that there are also more first
children. Personality is more important in
determining achievement than birth order.
Correlations between family size and socioeco-
nomic conditions also confuse the issue. In any
particular family, the best you can do is back
up your child's own personality. Middle or
second children can often use their competitive
feelings very successfully. Last children often
label themselves the "baby of the family" and
can continue to play that role right along.
Labels can become shelters to hide behind, or
they can be transcended.

QUESTION   Is there a statistical difference in the intelligence level of a first, second, and third child?

DR. BRAZELTON   Again, statistics won't help. What bothers parents is that they feel they may not be doing
enough for the later children. They forget that
the second learns from the first, the third learns
from the first two, and it all balances out.
Older children teach the younger ones so
much. If you don't feel guilty, which contrib-
utes to the child's own feeling of inadequacy,
you are more likely to see each child as an
individual.

QUESTION   Is it usual for the youngest child to be more
aggressive than the others? My youngest lords

The Considine Family

it over the other two. I have to protect them from him.

DR. BRAZELTON   Sometimes, a baby is overprotected from the older two by parents, especially if the older two are a "team." A mother will automatically take the baby's part. As the baby gets bigger, let the older two know that they can protect themselves. Meanwhile, I'd teach them how to take care of the baby and also how to express their negative, aggressive feelings about the baby safely to you. They don't need to like him all the time; they just need to know they will not be allowed to hurt him. You can help your older children learn about both sides of their feelings, the good and the bad. The idea is not to suppress these feelings but to learn about them.

QUESTION   How can I treat each child equally?

DR. BRAZELTON   You can't. Each one is a different personality and needs a different approach. The trouble is, it's exhausting to try to shift gears for each one. It makes a real difference to talk about their differences. I'd point out to one, "You like me to speak softly." To another, "You seem to need me to speak loudly." This eventually gives them insight into themselves. When they torture you with, "You are always nicer to him than you are to me," you can say, "You are very different people. I need to treat you differently. When I speak loudly to you, it's to make you listen, but I am speaking just as lovingly even if it's louder." If you don't get caught up in feeling guilty about the different feelings you have for each one, they needn't feel it either.

Middle Child

QUESTION   Is it all right to have favorites – "Daddy's girl"
            and "Mommy's boy"?

DR. BRAZELTON There will never be a way to avoid such fa-
            voritism or clichés. They are timeless and
            didn't come into being with Freud. Certainly,
            there is an appeal to each parent from the child
            of the opposite sex. You will inevitably treat
            children differently because of this. What you
            must not do is devalue either sex. You will
            give your "Mommy's boy" a feeling for his
            own charm, his own individuality, which will
            reinforce a good self-image. Every little girl
            needs an admiring father to grow up to be a
            confident female. Every boy needs a mother
            who believes that he's *the* most attractive male,
            in order to develop a necessary belief in him-
            self.

The Considine Family

The Giant Step

~

OFFICE VISIT

DR. BRAZELTON Hello, Considines! Come in. Hi, Sarah. Hi, Becky. Let's have a look at you, Tommy. You don't like to lie down, do you?

Tommy had just learned to walk. He was now on a more equal footing with his sisters. I usually don't try to examine a child of this age on my examining table. I used Tommy's sisters to help me and examined him sitting on his mother's lap.

DR. BRAZELTON How's Becky doing?

SUSAN Now Becky mothers Tommy more than Sarah does. Instead of following Sarah, she's now leading Tommy. She finally has someone to boss around. When they're playing, she'll do everything for him, so he hardly has a chance to develop skills on his own. She's smothering him. But she's better, just as you predicted.

Tommy struggled to get down, so I helped him. There has been a steady development of his gross motor movements – sitting, crawling, standing, now walking. Motor development is the most dramatic way an infant changes into a toddler. Tommy struggled to do things for himself, to join the others wherever they were.

DR. BRAZELTON There he goes! That's the way, Tommy!

The Giant Step

Tommy walked with a steady, determined, but wide-based gait. I watched to see what I could learn about him. Motor development is one of four lines of development I look at when I see a child in my office: cognitive, affective (emotional), social, and motor.

DR. BRAZELTON   He just can't stop. He keeps going every minute.

It was very hard for me to get him to sit still long enough to find out how his fine motor development was coming around. What I wanted him to do was shape his hand for an object as I moved it around. But he wasn't about to do that. He paid no attention. The main thing that I could see was an intense drive to "keep going." When I helped him down again from Susan's lap, he was leaning forward already before I could even get him on his feet, and then he was off! As he walked, he leaned forward. He was so eager to keep moving.

DR. BRAZELTON   Look how excited he is. It's as if he's telling us, "This is where I want to be!"

Being around two big sisters was pushing Tommy ahead. In order to keep up with them, getting around was to him the major job at this point. At the same time, he was learning a lot more: about independence, about object permanence (knowing that if he goes around the corner, Susan will still be there).

SUSAN   Are Sarah and Becky going to hold him back in his development because they are doing so much for him?

DR. BRAZELTON   Not Tommy. Just being a third child amounts to having tremendous stimulation. There is something new to watch or grab every minute.

SUSAN   Still, I feel guilty about how little time I spend with him compared to the girls when they

The Considine Family

were young. I paid so much attention to Sarah. Now I have to depend on the girls. When I hear Tommy in his playpen, and he's upset, I say, "Mommy has her hands up to here with soapsuds. Will somebody go do something for Tommy?" Sometimes, I place too much responsibility on them. They're only children.

Tommy's new walking seemed toward everyone else and away from Susan. Susan did not have enough time to enjoy her baby's "giant step."

DR. BRAZELTON Maybe you could siphon the two girls off onto their father sometimes and have a bit of time with him. Then you could give him special attention. Even once a week might be enough.

SUSAN That might help. Usually, I'm all over the place, frantic all the time. I can't keep up with everybody. They're all doing three different things, all at the same time.

DR. BRAZELTON I know just what you mean. I even feel chaotic having them all here in the office. But they are growing nicely. Just don't get pregnant again too soon.

SUSAN I'll wait a while.

But she didn't. A year later came Daniel.

THE ISSUES

When babies first walk, their whole world changes. Every parent is waiting for this event. It symbolizes successful entry into childhood. Mothers compare notes on when their babies walk, as if it were a sign of intelligence. Actually, it is more likely to be tied to temperament, for an intensely active, driving child will walk earlier than a quiet, thoughtful one. In any case, anxiety builds in parents' minds if their one-year-old is not walking. The average age for walking in our country is just over twelve months, but parents are eager to see their child walk earlier. It is as if it were a competitive thing: "My child must be the first to walk in the neighborhood."

With walking, children's ideas about themselves change. They are no longer dependent. They are ready for decision making on a grand scale. They can decide whether to go away from parents and whether to return. They can decide whether to round a corner and let mother get out of sight. She is no longer solely in control. This new sense of autonomy is overpowering. No wonder temper tantrums begin soon after walking. How can a child make such mammoth decisions without a struggle? Consider an eighteen-month-old boy trying to decide about something. His face screws up, his body tenses, he throws himself to the ground to flail and wail. The agony of his decision calls adults to him, but their efforts only fuel his struggle. It's *his* struggle! Walking has given him a whole new sense of his own power and of his ability to conquer the world around him. He wants to do it all himself, but as soon as he starts out he is faced with his need for dependence. He is becoming aware of a powerful ambivalence – will I or won't I, do I want to or don't I? This kind of ambivalence will color the rest of his life.

Walking fuels cognitive capacities as well. Children now have the capacity to check whether someone is still there, even though they themselves have gone into another room. They know that daddy and mommy will return at the end of the day, and they begin to wait for the sound of their footsteps. They can find toys left around the corner. Their sense of causality, of how things work, is growing.

In spite of their eagerness to see their child reach this milestone, all parents mourn the baby who has passed into toddlerhood. The incredible love affair of the first year is coming to an end. The struggle for the independence of the second year begins. Teasing for limits, pushing parents to punishments they'd have never believed themselves capable of, begins with walking. Parents must face this struggle and the need for setting limits. The second year

The Considine Family

is fraught with negativism, with provocative behavior which demands their active participation. Parents miss the delightful reciprocal relationship of the first year, and call this period the "terrible twos." But the opportunity for enormous and rapid spurts in every developmental line — motor, cognitive, emotional, social — is made possible by the toddler's ability to walk alone.

At around this time most children are waking up once or twice each night. They pull themselves up to stand and scream during each REM, or light sleep, cycle every three or four hours. They act as if they can't get back down alone. Everyone in the household pays a price for this particular step.

At birth, infants are programmed to be upright and to walk, an inborn reflex which provides a base for this voluntary activity later. At five months, when they are pulled up by the hands, they come to their feet with a burning desire to be upright that shows on their faces. A child practices, works, and struggles to walk for months before finally daring the first step. At that moment, the pleasure on a baby's face, reflected in the parents' faces and back again, registers the importance of this amazing achievement.

COMMON QUESTIONS

QUESTION   At what point should you begin to get concerned that your child is not walking?

DR. BRAZELTON   It depends on the type of child. For instance, is he rather flexible in the joints, what I call "flop-jointed"? Can you bend his joints beyond 180 degrees? These flop-jointed children have a lot to overcome. Later, this limberness becomes an asset, and they often become athletes. They have to master rather unstable hip and knee joints, and it takes longer. But there are other reasons for walking late. A quiet, thoughtful child who is not driven to perform

The Giant Step

motorically may walk late. He just watches and watches. A third or fourth child may be used to having everyone do things for him, so he sits and orders others around. Also, every time he stands and gets up his courage to venture forth, someone whirls by to unsettle him. That holds him back. If a child isn't walking by eighteen months, I'd worry. If he isn't pulling up to stand by twelve to fourteen months, you might be sure his legs are flexible, his hips are not dislocated, and his muscles aren't too flaccid. All of this is part of routine check-ups, which he should be having.

QUESTION   Is there any correlation between motor development and cognitive development?

DR. BRAZELTON   Not really. A quiet, thoughtful child can be smarter but late in walking. A child who walks early may not be spending as much time thinking as a quiet one who walks late. They are investing in different lines of development. The energy that goes into spurts in one line of development may not be available at that point to the other. There *is* a correlation, however, between cognitive learning and the ability to move around. Reaching for an object, a five-month-old baby begins to develop the concept of object permanence. Also, as she walks, a toddler begins to test "person permanence." If she walks around a corner, will her mother still be there? So, motor development is entwined with cognitive and social development in subtle ways.

QUESTION   My baby is interested in standing and not crawling. Should I encourage him to crawl?

The Considine Family

DR. BRAZELTON There's no reason to worry if the child does not crawl and prefers standing. Some children never crawl, and it doesn't matter to them at all. The myth that a child should crawl before he walks or he won't learn properly came from work with impaired children. Patterning them to crawl was seen to help them learn other things later on. There is no parallel in this with normal children.

QUESTION Does keeping a baby in a playpen interfere with motor development?

DR. BRAZELTON A playpen serves the parent's purposes of leaving an active child in a safe place. It can be frustrating to the child, but it's harmful only if the child is kept in one for too long. Actually, most children learn to cruise around and walk safely in them. So they help in practicing to walk.

QUESTION At what age is there emphasis on finger-thumb manipulation?

DR. BRAZELTON At about eight months, a child will begin to make a pincer out of her forefinger and thumb. I suggest allowing the child to start using her fingers to pick up soft bits of finger food at this time. This encourages and rewards her for her new achievement.

QUESTION When should I start to teach a child to use a fork and spoon?

DR. BRAZELTON At about sixteen months, he will be pretty good at it. Before that, a child manipulates utensils and learns how to use them over a

The Giant Step

long period. Children learn by imitation, by watching you.

QUESTION   Should I force my daughter to use her right hand?

DR. BRAZELTON   You should never force a child to use her right hand. Hand preference is related to the child's brain organization, and you can only confuse her, not help her, by pushing it. About 30 percent of children are either left-handed or have mixed dominance. You should respect her preference. A right-handed parent automatically pushes a child toward right-handedness. Every time you hand her anything, you'll hand it across to her right hand. If she doesn't pick up on it, don't push her.

QUESTION   Do older siblings encourage a child to learn to walk faster?

DR. BRAZELTON   Older children teach a younger child how to do many things. Walking is likely to be one of them. A younger child tries hard to please his older siblings.

QUESTION   My daughter likes to travel around in a walker. Does that cut down on her motivation to learn to walk?

DR. BRAZELTON   Yes, a walker can actually hold back a child's learning to walk by being a convenient support. At the time when they'd still be on the ground, learning by frustration, the walker does it for them. It removes the incentive. Frustration can be a powerful force for learning.

The Considine Family

QUESTION   Is walking learned?

DR. BRAZELTON   Walking is partly learned and partly a programmed behavior. A newborn baby already
has walking reflexes, which set the future program. These reflexes go underground when
voluntary behaviors take over. The reflex pattern of walking is lost by four to five months
of age, when a baby learns to come to a stand.
Then the reflex comes back again in the more
complex voluntary form of walking.

The Considine Family Revisited

࿔

Susan and Tom chose a time for me to visit them when the older three children were in bed for their naps. "That way we can concentrate on you," they assured me. "I'd like to concentrate on all of you as a family," I replied, but I knew what they were saying. When the children were up, they, as parents, were totally absorbed. Each child is a different individual, and their parents are intent upon reinforcing their children's individuality. They spend a lot of time thinking about their children, figuring out what makes them function. They are a family-oriented couple.

Tom's successful computer business is shaped around his family, rather than vice versa. He comes home early every evening to play with his children. He thinks twice about appointments and contacts that might take him away from home too much. He participates with Susan in some of the housework and in child care. As a result, Tom and Susan have real respect for each other. As I talk to them, each turns to the other repeatedly – for support, for approval, for confirmation of the thoughts they are sharing with me. I find them typical of a new kind of family. They are dedicated, certain of their priorities, and hungry for the kind of information about child development that will help them make choices. They know where they are going, and they expect to be successful.

Susan told me that she had begun to think about returning to work as an artist and a toy designer again, but she was going to wait a few more years. She loved being at home. She left her job at a publishing house eight years ago, but they still call her often for special assignments. She turns them down regularly, but they assure her that she still has opportunities waiting. She proudly showed me around their house, decorated with examples of her art, all now aimed at enriching her children's lives. She and her daughters draw and sew together every day. She makes their outfits for holidays, Halloween, Christmas, and Easter. I have the feeling that the girls may share her artistic inclinations. As she speaks of their times together sewing or drawing, her voice becomes softer, more girlish, and she glows with pleasure.

I asked whether Tommy (now three and a half) and Daniel (one year old) try to take part. "Tommy's his own person. He really resists being included as one of the mob. When we try to do something as a family, we find Tommy silently but doggedly pursuing his own track."

As if on cue, we heard a thud from upstairs. It sounded as if Tommy had fallen out of bed. No cry came. Tom went upstairs to see what had happened. He returned, grinning, "You know, you can hardly help Tommy." He had slipped over the side of his big bed onto the floor. He wasn't hurt, but it had frightened him. However, he did not want any help from his father, and he had mastered it all by himself; "I'm OK, I'm OK," he said.

He is certainly a self-sufficient little boy, and I wondered how much this might be in response to "too many mothers" – Susan, Sarah, and Becky. All three had hovered over Tommy as a baby and a toddler. When I brought this up, Susan remembered that Becky and Sarah had handled their sibling rivalry by competing for him. When Daniel came along, both girls turned to the new baby and, in the process, left Tommy on his own. So he withdrew, into his own resources. Now, Becky hovers over Daniel the way she did over Tommy. The two girls dress the boys up in their mother's costumes. The boys alternate between being Robin Hood, a mean robber, the dog in the Wizard of Oz, or a witch. Their play is dominated by their older sisters' imaginations. Tommy's real retreat is to his "school." He pressed his mother to let him go to day care twice a week. When Daniel presides in his mother's lap, Tommy has been displaced there, too. So his refuge is school.

Susan is amazed at the baby's dependence – greater than that of any of the other three. Actually, as I saw it, his dependence is an escape from the pressure of active family and two hovering sisters, coupled with a determined kind of hold on Susan. Tommy maintains his independence by removing himself. Danny maintains his by quietly but firmly manipulating his parents. He is not overtly demanding, nor is he so intrusive that they must constantly attend

The Considine Family Revisited

to him. But he keeps them interacting with him at some less-than-conscious level. They touch him, handle him, cuddle him while they talk. But they hardly look at him. And they don't speak to him. To them, he is almost like a "lovey," a plaything, while they concentrate on the two girls or on their conversation with me. Occasionally, they look down at him in response to a sound, but it is the girls who still dominate their thinking.

I asked Susan how it had worked out with Becky. She assured me that the "middle child" issue was no longer a real problem, that having discussed it with me had been a help. I had helped her realize how deeply she identified with Becky. Becky had a combination of a drive and a deep fear of failure, which drove her to try to live up to her older sister. Sarah had been so competent that, even when she was a baby, Tom's mother had warned Susan that Sarah could easily run the family. Indeed, Sarah had trained herself. She'd learned to sleep through the night "all on her own," Susan said. "It was almost as if she didn't need me. But Becky did. It felt good, and I could see myself and my own struggles in her. I like to be needed by these kids. Becky shows me that she does. Becky waked longer at night. She resisted toilet training. She could sit on the can doggedly for hours, blaming her bodily functions as if they were a person. 'Pee won't come down. My b.m. is just not ready. Sorry.' Susan remembers how she got a real charge out of Becky's kind of thinking, and that they continue to communicate in a collegial way. They are more like peers than mother and daughter. When a problem arises with the boys, Susan and Becky discuss what needs to be done. Becky hovers over the boys like a surrogate mother; indeed, her "middle child" syndrome turned her into one, into a total identification with Susan in her mothering role. It almost seems as if she needs to outdo Susan by taking possession of the boys at times.

How does Tommy take all this mothering? "He's so different from the girls. He's happy. He's physically strong and very cool. He makes up his mind when he's ready to do something, and does it. No one really influences him. Becky can't get beyond his independent coolness any more than I can. He likes being fussed over by all us girls, but he sure can take it or leave it. He wouldn't even sit on the toilet until he was three; then, he trained himself in one day. When he wanted to walk, he got up and did it. He calls the baby 'my buddy Danny.' I think he'll line Danny up to help him combat against the girls someday, but he doesn't need him now. He just manages on his own. When they dress him up, he lets them. Then he takes over. The other day, they dressed him up in a bathrobe and jewelry and called him a prince. He walked solemnly away from their game. He came in to me and said, 'Guess who I am now? I'm the Prince. Is the Prince's dinner ready?'"

"If Becky has managed her feelings of desertion by becoming like you," I asked, "and Tommy avoids it by being independent, what will Danny do if you have another baby?"

"I won't! I've told Tom he'll have to have the next one, and no other woman would have him with all this baggage. We're through having babies. I want to go back to work some day."

"You're giving up on Tom's family pattern of eleven children?" I asked. They both nodded vigorously. "Oh, yes, we are!"

Susan said, "My mother died three years ago. My sister works full-time. My father has multiple myeloma and lives with my brother now, but I may be needed. I've got enough responsibility. If I were younger (she's thirty-four), I'd have more. Wanting more is partly selfish. I have so much fun with these kids. I love making chocolate chip cookies with them. I don't want to ever stop. But I also want to be involved with each of them at every level. If I had too many, I wouldn't be able to. It frustrates me now to give up any part of the bringing up, to school or anywhere else. I want to savor every single minute with them. The other day, my publishers called to offer me a job, only part-time. But I said, 'Not yet, I'm having too good a time with these kids.'"

Tom looked at her with appreciation, perhaps also envy. He said, "I get home as early as I can in the afternoon. I want to join in the fun. I brought my computer home a week ago so I could work here. But I can't. All I can do is play computer games with the kids. They have learned so much in a week, I can hardly believe it." He showed me the games they played and the drawings the girls had made which he'd stored on his computer. It looked to me as if the computer was becoming a part of the family. Tom was as proud of their developing skills with the instrument of his profession as he was of his own success.

The Considine Family Revisited

I wondered how Tom had learned to be so easy about participating at home and with his children. I asked how he'd grown up. He said he was in the middle of the eleven children in his family. He'd grown up on a farm and had always been immersed in animals and in his large family. Although he had retreated into his books instead of helping his mother with his smaller siblings, he guessed he'd always observed her out of the corner of his eye, and so wanted a family of his own. Did his father help with them? "When we were older and more interesting, but not when we were babies." Both he and Susan look very young, although they are in their mid-thirties. Their close identification with their children seems to affect their appearance as well as their behavior. They seemed so interdependent. It was a pleasure to be with them as we talked about the goals they had for their family.

At this point, Tommy hit the floor upstairs again. I wanted to see how he had reacted, and why he hadn't called out for help. Although I went quickly up the stairs with his parents following calmly behind me, he was already back in bed, cuddled in and asleep before we got there. Susan and Tom nodded appreciatively at each other, saying, "That's Tommy."

Susan showed me around the three little bedrooms upstairs, full of her artwork. There were sewn, quilted figures of children and flowers, and stenciling to decorate the walls. As we entered the girls' bedroom, where they had been napping, I could see that Susan's drawings of children were replicas of her two little girls. They are somewhat overwhelming in their picturesqueness. As I admired these two, who seemed delighted to see me, Susan said (as if reading my mind), "They may look alike, but they're not. Sarah is self-confident, always sure of what she wants. She never makes a demand. She's at the top of her class. Becky is more like me, having to struggle for every step. Do you remember when Tommy came, and she felt herself in danger, how she had aches and pains? She lisped, then had a mild stammer. Finally, she found a better way to get attention, by imitating me as I handle the boys. With help, she learned to conquer her pains and her speech and got more and more confident. She feels good about herself now. She's independent of Sarah, and she's started to become her own person."

The Considine Family

The girls wanted to show me their "work." They rushed me downstairs to the computer. At the ages of six and eight, and after only a week of exposure, they were already competent enough to retrieve their own pictures, their own games. They felt like experts already, and they were delighted to see that I was in such awe of them. I secretly wondered whether such an appealing instrument mightn't absorb some of the energy they might otherwise use on social relationships, for reading, learning sports, and for other kinds of learning. Their utter absorption reminded me of the kind of "hooked" attention children show in front of the television set. This technology carries with it a tremendous opportunity for exploring and learning about whole new worlds. But it can be at a price. Machines with such power are both seductive and demanding. When they are coupled with parental involvement and parental approval, they must be virtually irresistible to a developing child. As parents we are responsible for making sure our children's lives maintain some balance and that we don't contribute to a narrow precocity in their intellectual development, which could lead to burnout later on.

For these girls, computer games were also a way to capture their father. They kept his interest and attention by learning more and more. They identified with him and his "work." They could engage him in games, almost on his level. And, best of all, they could exclude Susan. If she wants to get back into the Oedipal triangle, she'll have to learn their language. It will be interesting to see whether she will, for she and they have another means of communication – art and sewing. It will also be fascinating to see how the boys will respond to the parents' two modes for capturing and communicating with the children. Watching this close-knit, talented family, as they sort out their evolving relationships, has been a real privilege.

The Sheehan-Weber Family

৵

CHAPTER IV

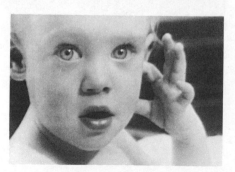

The Sheehan-Weber Family

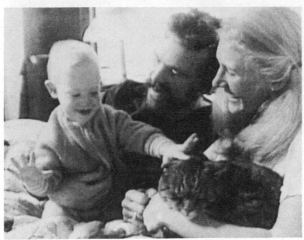

The Sheehan-Weber Family

Family History

ॐ

Mark Weber and Franci Sheehan had been married for two years before Adrienne was conceived. They had already endured two unsuccessful pregnancies – a tubal pregnancy and a miscarriage at twenty weeks. The obstetrician assured Franci that there was no reason to think that this would happen again and encouraged her to try once more. Mark, tall and handsome, is a psychiatric social worker. Franci, a tall, good-looking blond, is an obstetric nurse practitioner. Both of them had always wanted a family. Their own parents each had three children. Franci's father, a successful mid-western businessman, adored his tow-headed little girl. At night he'd read her Golden Books about "Nurse Nancy." By the time she was five she had made up her mind to become a nurse, and she never deviated. Today she feels very fortunate to have always known what she wanted. Mark was the youngest. He had always looked up to his older brother, who, at the age of eighteen, had had a schizophrenic breakdown. The family was overwhelmed by such a seemingly unexplainable tragedy. When Mark was a teenager he decided to go into mental health, determined to prevent such an experience from occurring in other families. When Franci and Mark met they were in graduate school and pursuing their own careers. They were, at twenty-eight and twenty-nine, well along, and met one night on a blind date. Once they began to match career goals and realize how serious the other was, it was a foregone conclusion. "That was it," said Franci. "I told Mark that I didn't want to fool around. I wanted a family. He did, too, and asked me to marry him. It was as simple as that! We both wanted the same things – careers in mental health and a family. We've never wanted anything else."

After Mark and Franci had been married for two years, having a baby became an obsession, and Franci became pregnant again. She was checked frequently because of her earlier miscarriage. Her cervix was found to be dilated, "an incompetent cervix" said the doctor, and she was placed on bedrest. She remembers being terrified. She knew she might have a premature infant. If she did, she desperately hoped that it would survive and that she could somehow hang on until it did. The Sheehan-Webers were professionals in the health field, but even knowing as much as they did was no help here and now. Both were aware of all of the dangers involved in prematurity – brain damage, blindness, chronic lung disease – and were constantly preoccupied with thoughts on how to prolong Franci's pregnancy. They saw every unexpected event as a threat to it, so they stayed home, just hanging on. "The baby and I would sort of talk to each other," said Franci. "We were going to make this and we were going to hold out as long as we could. I felt I had a lot of attachment to her before she was born."

At twenty-five weeks, four months too early, Franci's membranes ruptured spontaneously. Infection was suspected and so she was delivered of a 700 gram (1½-pound), 13-inch girl.* The baby was one of the smallest prematures to ever survive at Boston's Beth Israel Hospital at that time. At the moment of her birth Adrienne was rushed off to the neonatal intensive care unit. There, given oxygen, put on a respirator, and surrounded by masses of monitoring equipment, she seemed lifeless, and Franci was convinced that she could not be revived, that she would never see her "alive" again. Adrienne was given the usual Apgar test – to judge her condition at birth – but her score was only one out of a possible ten points. But she was resuscitated successfully, and, just a nameless handful of a baby, she began to breathe on her own. Already she showed the kind of spunk that would mark her stormy course later on in life.

Mark was present at delivery, but when he saw how tiny and immature his baby daughter was, he telephoned their two families to tell them that she probably wouldn't live. He and Franci clung desperately to each other, preparing each other for the loss that appeared to be imminent. Adrienne was then transferred to Chil-

---

* Adrienne's stormy course is documented in *Born Early: The Story of a Premature Baby* by Mary Ellen Avery, M.D., and Georgia Litwack (Boston: Little, Brown, 1983). For parents, it is one of the most helpful books about premature infants.

Family History

dren's Hospital where she would spend the next twelve weeks. Within a few days she began to flail around a little, to grasp and to struggle. "When I saw her move like that," said Mark, "she gave me hope – for the first time!" He told me how, in the tiny incubator, she had intravenous tubes in her head and her arms and an oxygen mask on her nose and mouth, as well as wires all over her chest to monitor her heartbeat.

"Luckily, I didn't know as much then as I've learned since," said Franci. "I really didn't know that much about preemies. My master's was in obstetrics – maternal child nursing. They hadn't really ever exposed me to a preemie nursery, or to what those babies face, or I'd have been terrified. Mark and I were so glad to have a baby at all, after that first terrible pregnancy and death, that the mere fact that Adrienne was alive at all was like a gift. I just put my mind to work on helping her survive. It never really occurred to me until later that there was a danger of brain damage. It was much harder for Mark. He had taken classes in childbirth, and he was really geared up for the whole show. Cutting the pregnancy short and missing a normal delivery was a terrible deprivation. He did worry about Adrienne's brain and her condition. I denied it. Maybe I was protecting myself. Now I read about preemies and I feel so, so lucky."

Adrienne was no larger than Mark's outstretched hand, but they both admired her tiny perfection. "She had Mark's nose and my hands." After they'd spent a few days looking at her, experiencing with her her struggle to live, they dared to name her – a family name, "Adrienne." They even dared to begin to think of her as a baby, maybe even one who would grow up. But as soon as they left her side, their doubts and fears returned. Franci remembers that when she went home from the hospital without her baby she wept almost constantly. All the doctors and nurses told her it was not her fault, but she remembered the expression, "incompetent cervix," and she felt as though it were she herself who was incompetent as a childbearing person. "The day I left the hospital was the worst day of my life. It seemed to me like nothing had gone right, one loss after another. I did not dare hope that this child would live." Mark was more positive, and he tried to hold Franci together with his good humor. "Adrienne's prematurity meant that I got to see her that much earlier," said Mark, trying to rationalize the situation.

Every blood test, every report, gave them hope, as they desperately tried to hang on, to keep in touch with her. "When another baby died in the nursery we were afraid Adrienne might be next. I'd never had such a hard thing in my life to adjust to, and I'm not sure I did it very well," Franci explained. "We were numb. We tried to live as normal a life as possible, but our souls and our minds were in that premature nursery." They didn't dare send out birth announcements. They hated having relatives or friends call them up for news of her, because it meant facing their fears all over again. They withdrew into themselves. At times, they could hardly even communicate with each other, so great was their terror. "We just lived from day to day." At other times they found themselves getting angry with each other – irrationally. Later, their professional backgrounds helped them recognize this as part of the grief reaction they were going through, but at the time they were not immune to feelings of "Why me?"

During the next two weeks the baby had to be fed intravenously, apparently due to a bowel obstruction. This complication alone could have killed her. She developed the severe jaundice of a premature baby whose liver and kidneys are too immature to discharge the blood-breakdown products that build up after birth. Jaundice can impair a baby's brain, and Franci knew that. Adrienne had to be given phototherapy. For days she lay still under the strong lights. Although they covered her eyes, these lights were a source of added worry. So was the possibility of retrolental fibroplasia, an eye condition due to excessive oxygen, which can progress to blindness in prematures. Franci had been given injections before the birth, so the baby's lungs were protected from the threat of hyaline membrane disease, common in extreme prematurity. Another danger for prematures is hemorrhage within the skull. A brain scan determined that this had not occurred, and the Sheehan-Webers began to hope – not only that their baby might recover but that, by some real miracle, she might even be healthy and completely normal. Nevertheless, as both Mark and Franci remember, they never dared to talk to each other about the fear they both had that Adrienne's brain was damaged. It was just too frightening.

Family History

To help keep her temperature constant, Adrienne had to wear a hat. Franci knitted and embroidered one for her. She used a tennis ball to make it the right size.

Twelve weeks later Adrienne weighed nearly three pounds. They transferred her back to the less-stressful nursery where she had been born. Mark and Franci were elated. They were almost out of the woods. Each new step gave them hope, such as the day Adrienne was put into a crib. Franci and Mark visited her every day and watched her every move. "We studied every reaction, every grimace. We tried desperately to get to know her as a person. When she'd turn to our voices, we'd say, 'She knows us!' When we picked her up, she seemed to nestle into our arms. We took every movement as a sign of her being healthy – always hoping, trying to balance our fears with hope."

At sixteen weeks, one week after her due date, Adrienne weighed four pounds, four ounces and was considered stable enough to go home to her by then yearning parents. Her eyes, her brain, her behavior now all checked out normal. But Franci and Mark faced a whole new set of anxieties, for they found themselves now totally responsible for her well-being. The rewards, however, were greater now. Adrienne could smile at them. She could turn her head toward their voices. She could look into their eyes and follow their faces. She was becoming "their baby" at last. While she was in the hospital they both felt so tense with each other that each would visit Adrienne alone, "to avoid competition." Now, they were able to care for her together. She was such a responsibility, they each needed the other. Their competitive feelings were turned into mutual support – stress had become a kind of cement to hold the family together.

Overload

ॐ

OFFICE VISIT

All three Sheehan-Webers arrived in the office, looking a little weary. Adrienne was now eighteen months.

DR. BRAZELTON   How are you all doing?

MARK   OK, except that Adrienne seems cranky these days. When I get home around 5, that seems to be the time that Adrienne cries a lot.

DR. BRAZELTON   Does she seem to fall apart?

MARK   Exactly. At just the wrong time. I've been waiting all day to get to her, and she's too upset to do anything with me.

FRANCI   It's hard on all of us. I've had her all day and I really want the relief when Mark comes home. Mark's had a hard day, and he comes in and I give him this cranky, crying baby. He begins to feel it's his fault.

DR. BRAZELTON   Every day, every baby must process a staggering bombardment of brand-new data. Overload happens quickly. Faster than for a grown-up. The child shuts off, or blows up. Adrienne's not really out of control; the crying is a way of regulating herself.

MARK   But how can I make our time together better?

DR. BRAZELTON   The main thing is not to take it personally. You're her father, you feel torn away from her all day, anyway, not in on what's happening. I always felt sort of jealous of my wife, having all the best moments. Of course, *she* never saw it that way at all!

MARK   That's true.

DR. BRAZELTON   If you feel like you've missed everything, when you get home you try to make up for this, and that's the time she breaks down. It's very hard. It's even harder when your child is premature and extra sensitive to overstimulation. The problem of overload continues much longer for these children.

FRANCI   She starts getting excited even before Mark gets home.

DR. BRAZELTON   Maybe you should just have a martini when you get there, and let off steam while she does, too! But seriously, with some babies, once you let them fall apart, you can soothe them again and then they become charming. When this happens next, try putting her down to cry for a little while; then pick her up and you may have a better time with her. It's hard for her, too. She's really trying to protect herself and learning to balance between needing a break and participating in excitement. If she lets herself get too overloaded, she has to fall apart.

FRANCI   Do you think it would be helpful to try to change her nap schedule so that she wouldn't be so cranky when Mark comes home?

The Sheehan-Weber Family

DR. BRAZELTON Maybe. When does she take her nap?

FRANCI In the morning.

DR. BRAZELTON She doesn't nap in the afternoon?

FRANCI Not usually after 12.

DR. BRAZELTON Maybe you could sit down with her at about 2 or 3 and just rock her, or give her a good calming-down period.

FRANCI She might like that.

DR. BRAZELTON But I want you to feel encouraged. The main thing I feel about her today is how well she is doing, how far you've come from the raw, little, over-reactive baby who fell apart every time you whispered. Of course, that comes from what you have already done to help her learn to calm herself down. It's exciting to see her progress.

THE ISSUES

Every infant constantly gets and must react to stimuli. Each stimulus sets up a chain of reactions through which the baby experiences her environment. Each new experience adds to the last, and the newborn's nervous system is largely at the mercy of her stimulus-response systems. In order to react to – and learn from – all of this bombardment, the infant must have a predetermined ability to select out "appropriate" over "inappropriate" signals. The full-term infant in the delivery room does indeed seem to have some definite preferences and dislikes. She can make choices by shutting out disturbing stimuli. She protects herself against overstimulation.

Overload

She is also able to suppress within herself her disturbing reactions to stimuli outside.

In this way, babies avoid the dangers of overload. The threshold, the point at which a baby is overloaded, differs from one individual to another. A stressed, or overloaded, baby has many ways to "turn off": entering a sleep-like state; yawning; eyes that seem to float, stare off into the distance, or be covered by a sort of membrane; arms and shoulders that hang limply; a deep, regular, and relentless breathing, like that of an exhausted adult.

In premature babies, these defenses are not as well developed, and the dangers of overload are accentuated. In an immature, disorganized brain, each bit of stimulation – auditory, visual, tactile, or kinesthetic (movement) – only acts to overwhelm the baby's nervous system, still too raw to learn from stimuli. The trick for the parents, of either premature or very sensitive babies, is to find the right level of stimulation, so that the baby can start the process of learning, of adapting to the environment, and of becoming organized enough to receive, register, and react to experiences. This is not easy. It is complicated by the baby's prior experience in the premature nursery, which very likely was overwhelming. This early overload sets up in a baby defenses that are frustrating to the parents. When they look for a response from her, she may withdraw automatically. I worry that parents take this as failure on their part and develop feelings of rejection. Sometimes parents switch. They provide too little stimulation. Lack of stimulation is more devastating than overstimulation, and it can seriously interfere with a baby's development and growth.

Parents of full-term babies always know when they have made a hit, for a pair of alert eyes, or a smile, or a turned head tells them so. Similarly, there are very few parents of full-term babies who fail to get the opposite message when their baby cries, or actively tries to squirm away from them. The reactions of preemies are necessarily more subtle, and parents need to be shown what those subtle behaviors that say "I've had enough" are. In our Child Development Unit, we learned how to work with these families. We showed them how, slowly and quietly, using one kind of stimulation at a time, to look at, talk to, touch, or pick up the baby. But only one thing at a time. Only as the baby registers her

The Sheehan-Weber Family

ability to take in and assimilate one activity, do we add another. There comes a point when the baby demonstrates by her behavior that she's had enough. Then parents learn to pull back and to stop. There will always be another time. Learning to handle this kind of hypersensitivity is a long-term endeavor, but perhaps the most critical lesson for parents of easily overloaded babies to learn.

One common response to an overloaded nervous system is a crying period at the end of the day. This occurs regularly in full-term babies. In prematures it seems to occur after they have reached a certain stage of maturity – often at about forty-six weeks (gestational age, meaning from conception). Paradoxically, in them, it is a sign of maturity. At the end of an active day the nervous system has reached its limit. It has taken in and handled all the stimuli it can from the world outside. It just seems to "blow" – with an hour or two of almost inconsolable, but predictable, crying. The baby will calm down if she is handled, carried, or fed frequently. But when she's returned to her bed, she starts fussing again, until she's all fussed out. Too much handling and anxious stimulation from caregivers may create even more excessive crying. It occurs more easily in an immature baby, who takes a longer time to learn how to handle incoming stimuli and organize her states of consciousness (awake, alert, sleep, and crying states) through a twenty-four-hour period. As a baby grows and matures, this crying period gradually decreases, and she learns how to discharge her end-of-the-day tension in other ways. In full-term babies, the crying ends at ten to twelve weeks; in prematures, as we have seen with Adrienne, it can take much longer. Parents feel like failures until they understand that they can help the baby handle it if they develop a routine for her end-of-the-day crying periods. The routine I recommend is as follows:

1 Try to find a reason for the crying and satisfy yourself that nothing will readily stop it.

2 Calm down and force yourself to quit fussing over the child.

3 If it is a young baby, put her down for ten minutes at a time. Let her fuss for that period, then pick her up, hold and

"contain" her, feed her sugar water or water, and bubble her. If she is still jumpy and itchy, put her down to fuss for another ten minutes, then repeat the cycle. At the point where you think she's cried it all out, swaddle her, or place her on her abdomen to let her go to sleep. She may need a milk feeding before you put her to bed. If so, feed her in a quiet, darkened room and soothe her afterward. Until she's ready, this won't work, so you'll have to learn to read her cues.

4 If the child is older, try leaving her alone for a while, then introduce one quiet activity at a time. Try for quick periods, even if the child does not nap. Before meals, bedtime, or a family time together, try to institute familiar, soothing routines, such as reading, rocking, or music. Watch for cues of overload.

COMMON QUESTIONS

QUESTION   What exactly is overload? Does it happen with all babies?

DR. BRAZELTON   All children have a threshold, above which they can't take more activity or stimulation. Overload is simply when you go past that threshold.

QUESTION   How can you prevent it?

DR. BRAZELTON   You can't and shouldn't try to prevent it completely. A baby learns a lot from being somewhat over-stimulated and finding that she can calm herself down. But I wouldn't let a sensitive baby be greatly overwhelmed at the end of the day; try to be quieter and more soothing.

The Sheehan-Weber Family

QUESTION

Do you think that very active parents tend to over-stimulate their children? My husband is very active and tends to play with our son in a very rough and excited way.

DR. BRAZELTON

Active parents do tend to over-stimulate their babies. Perhaps they are unconsciously trying to shape their baby to be like themselves. Also, there may be a genetic predisposition for your son to have the same kind of temperament as your husband. Don't fight it!

QUESTION

I like to play with our three-year-old daughter when I get home from work. Is there a problem with over-stimulating her before bedtime?

DR. BRAZELTON

This play is very important to her; go ahead and enjoy it in your own way. Sure, you'll get her jazzed up. But then save some time afterward. Try to set up some rocking or soothing routine to help her calm back down so she can get off to sleep.

QUESTION

My son was premature and he seems to withdraw when I play with him. Does he need more stimulation?

DR. BRAZELTON

Some immature babies just seem to withdraw. Some babies are ready to interact, yet others need to be led into ways of being interactive. Try to watch him for the cues of being overloaded, but then, within his tolerance level, do play with him and try to draw him out.

QUESTION

Are there dietary factors which influence over-stimulation? Can sugar make a child hyperactive?

Overload

DR. BRAZELTON   I believe that diet is a minor factor, not as important as some people believe. But with certain kinds of sensitive and hyperactive children, the rapid rise and fall of insulin levels that follow ingestion of sugars, such as candy, can make a difference. They may get more active after eating sweets. If so, I'd try to limit them. Later, a child can understand this and take responsibility. It's not easy when everyone around you is eating them.

QUESTION   When grandparents come to visit, my three children get very excited. What can parents do to prevent this?

DR. BRAZELTON   I'm not sure that the parent should try to prevent over-stimulation in this situation. It's pretty exciting when grandparents come to visit. Maybe you had just better enjoy it. Grandparents should be exciting for children. Far too few children see enough of their grandparents these days. Just plan for quieter times after they've gone. It's worth it.

QUESTION   What can a working parent do if another caregiver over-stimulates a baby or child?

DR. BRAZELTON   Some caregivers may be insensitive to the threshold of the child, or else unaware of the rhythms in threshold that vary with the time of day. For example, every baby's threshold is low at the end of the day. Either teach the caregiver your baby's cues to being overloaded, or else change caregivers. This kind of sensitivity to the baby would be the first thing I'd look for in a sitter or nanny.

The Sheehan-Weber Family

QUESTION   I worry about the lack of time and, therefore, stimulation I am able to give my third child. Do you have any suggestions?

DR. BRAZELTON   A third child is so lucky. They get so much from the older two. It's difficult for them to be under-stimulated. If you teach the older two how to play with her, you won't need to feel so guilty. No one enjoys trying to divide herself into three parts. Have a special time alone with your youngest from time to time.

QUESTION   Television seems to me an assault on the senses of a child. How do you recommend dealing with it?

DR. BRAZELTON   I'd set limits – for example, an hour a day for children up to five. They can choose what to watch, but that's the limit. Then, when you can, watch with them and discuss what you've seen. That makes it a rewarding family experience and helps children deal with scary or over-exciting programs.

A Sense of Self

OFFICE VISIT

Franci arrived in my office with Adrienne, now two years old. She is a slender, rather fragile-looking, child. Her blond hair is still wispy. Her expression is quite serious, although when she smiles her whole bearing seems softer, more slowed down. Most of the time she seems to be concentrating so intently on what she is doing that I feel I am being intrusive when I speak to her. In response, she seems suddenly to snap out of whatever she is doing. Her whole body almost jerks. I would wonder whether concentration wasn't still difficult for her, due to remnants of hypersensitivity left over from her prematurity. Perhaps, to concentrate, she had to use every ounce of energy she had. If there were a sudden loud noise, or a shift in someone's posture, she'd jump, almost imperceptibly, but it was obvious that she found it difficult to take in new situations. However, when she smiled, the contrast and the relief were so great, both for her and for me, that I found myself acting silly — to try to appeal to her. Of course, the more I pushed it, the more this sensitive two-year-old drew away from me.

DR. BRAZELTON   *To Adrienne.* You are a beautiful girl. *To Franci.* You said you've been worried about her ears. Have they been kicking up with infections?

FRANCI   She's been waking up a lot at night, pulling her ear; and I'm just concerned that she has another infection.

DR. BRAZELTON   Poor baby, you've had so much trouble, haven't you?

The Sheehan-Weber Family

To Franci, Adrienne's congenital ear blockage was just another reminder of the fact that a premature child is still in some ways different and inadequate.

DR. BRAZELTON   With prematures, the structure of the ear is narrow and small where the internal canals go into the throat, so that it tends to block up and get infected.

Meanwhile, I'm watching how she uses her hands, whether she shapes them appropriately as she reaches for a toy. I offer her a toy to test her. She refuses it.

DR. BRAZELTON   She sure is full of spunk. I suppose that's what helped her get through in the first place.

FRANCI   One of the things that I have a hard time with is knowing whether I'm supposed to be looking at her development according to when she should have been born, or at her real age.

DR. BRAZELTON   Well, I think with a preemie I'd never go by her real age. They catch up but not for a long, long time. While she is certainly catching up on skills with other children her age, you still have to ask how much is she overcoming to get to those skills? I think it's better to make allowances because a preemie has to do so much more work to get to the same place that another child would get to easily.

FRANCI   When you see people on the street, and they ask how old your child is, you never really know what to say.

As we talked, this wispy but intent little girl worked to put toys together and make them work. She had a few remnants of motor disorganization, due to the insult to her nervous system. She still walked with a wide-based gait, although, as she walked faster, and when she ran, her gait improved. As she put out her hand to grasp an object, I saw that she had an almost imperceptible tremor. It persisted as she concentrated on manipulating the toy. These soft signs of very minor motor imbalance (of flexor and extensor muscles) told me how hard she'd been working over the past year to organize her motor system. No wonder she frowned as she played!

DR. BRAZELTON I know just what you mean.

Her comment hid the deeper, more abiding question that resides in the heart of every pre-term mother – when will my baby be normal?

DR. BRAZELTON *To Adrienne (as I demonstrated how I'd look in her ear).* Now watch. I'm going to look in your ear. Can you look in my ear first? Now, I'll look in your ear. What a good girl!

FRANCI Every child gets ear infections, but you sort of feel, well, since I've been through so much with a premature, I shouldn't have to deal with all these normal things, too.

DR. BRAZELTON That's really interesting. You have this picture in your mind, left over from all those terrible times, of her as somehow different, so when she gets into a normal stage, you have to wrench yourself out of the old image. It must be twice as complicated and twice as hard. But, you know, all that attachment can make the outcome even more rewarding than a full-term pregnancy.

The Sheehan-Weber Family

Despite her light-hearted manner, Franci was still coping with feelings of failure. I sensed that she was still unfairly blaming herself.

FRANCI

One other thing that I've been worried about is her size. She's small, not as much in height but certainly in weight. She's still small for her age. Do you think she'll always be smaller than she would have been if she'd been full term?

DR. BRAZELTON

Well, it's hard for me to say because it has a lot to do with how much growth had gone on in the uterus before she was born. If it was normal growth up till then, the chances are she's going to have catch-up growth later on and will be a normal height. My guess, from looking at her, is that she's going to be built like you, though. She is going to be tall and lean and never will be a chubby, muscular little number. What you're asking is when can I compare her to everybody else around her. The truth is — probably never.

FRANCI

She is certainly as stubborn as any baby her age; in fact, maybe more so.

DR. BRAZELTON

Adrienne needed this stubborn strength just to survive. Next to survival, catching up is mere child's play. We know now that prematures learn differently when they get to school, and that it takes them a little bit longer to learn the same things that another child might learn very quickly. That doesn't mean that she isn't going to learn; she will. But it means that she's got to work harder to do it.

Mark comes in. Adrienne looks up to grin at him.

A Sense of Self

FRANCI   Look who's here.

MARK   What are you drawing? That's very good.

Adrienne has been drawing, as if to show off for us. Part of Adrienne's make-up seems to be a sensitivity to the approval of her parents. Although her need was hidden under a heavy layer of stubborn negativism, one could see how critical for her it was to get their approval of the hard work she had put into each new achievement.

FRANCI   I've taken Adrienne back to the hospital nurs-
          ery a couple of times, and whenever the nurses
          see her, if the mother of a preemie is there,
          they bring the mother out and say, "Look at
          this baby. This was a preemie, and look at her
          now." The mother always says, "Oh, I can't
          imagine that my baby is ever going to grow
          up and look like that."

Adrienne ran across the room. Franci was trying to see her child two ways – the way she is, and the way she, Franci, would like to see her.

FRANCI   People are always commenting that she's like
          a ballerina.

DR. BRAZELTON Yes. She's delicate and beautiful in the way she
          performs. She's overcome her awkwardness
          for the most part even though she still has a
          wide base when she walks.

Mark and Franci could handle complete honesty on my part. They know too much to deny a problem. There were subtle signs that Adrienne was still organizing her nervous system in order to overcome her immaturity. The parents needed support for the work they were doing to help her. To deny her problems would only

The Sheehan-Weber Family

make them unsure of their own observations. The anxiety was still there. It was better faced and dealt with.

DR. BRAZELTON   She's dancing as if to try to overcome her walking difficulties. She's doing it, too. Is she talking?

MARK   *To Adrienne.* Can you say "cat"? Where's Adrienne? *Adrienne points to herself.* There she is!

FRANCI   Do you think you can get the crayons back in the box? Where's the box? *To Dr. Brazelton.* She has a very stubborn streak, which I think has helped her as a premature baby; she had a lot of fight in her and a lot of desire to live. I can already sense that now there are going to be some battles as we get into disciplining and limit-setting.

Adrienne was stubborn and negative when she wasn't sure she could succeed. She delayed action until she'd assimilated both the request and her own awareness of how to respond to it.

DR. BRAZELTON   If you ask me, this is the most exciting moment: when a child begins to realize, "I can do it myself." *To Adrienne.* You don't want me to touch you at all, do you? *To Franci.* This autonomy that she showed me just then by pushing my hand away, this independence, is really so marvelous. *I was modeling for Franci, showing her how critical it was to let Adrienne do things her own way and at her own speed.*

FRANCI   Her independence in the last month or so is amazing. But it's been difficult, too, because she's been such an easy, compliant child and all of a sudden she's gotten so negative.

A Sense of Self

DR. BRAZELTON   Independence also means rebellion.

FRANCI   She's much more difficult to handle. When she gets negative, she starts hitting at me and I don't know how to handle that.

DR. BRAZELTON   This bothers you?

FRANCI   I feel like I need to tell her that she can't do that, but at the same time I don't think she understands what she's doing, so I don't know how to react.

DR. BRAZELTON   Well, I wouldn't either. I wouldn't do too much because it's important for her to be independent. I think hitting starts off not as something aggressive, but as something more exploratory. She is learning about you and about herself. Limits, though, are a critical part of that learning.

Adrienne trotted away, toward some toys.

DR. BRAZELTON   Does this give you a sense of loss, of giving up something you worked so hard over?

FRANCI   Yes! I had that same feeling when she stopped breast-feeding; I experienced it then. You don't know what I went through to be able to breast-feed, and I couldn't believe it when Adrienne wanted to stop. Now I feel that way about her becoming stubborn and independent. I really only went through about half of my pregnancy. You don't have the time in such a short pregnancy to get ready to detach. All you have is this feeling of something being taken away too soon. With a normal pregnancy, you have nine months to attach, and then you can be ready to detach at delivery.

DR. BRAZELTON   In the beginning you had to work so hard to get attached, so trying to let go now is very hard.

FRANCI   I try to let her have her independence; but I still worry about caring too much, or that I might be smothering her. It's something I have to think about all the time.

Faced with the independence of one baby, many mothers consider a new attachment.

DR. BRAZELTON   Do you want another baby?

FRANCI   Yes, but there is still so much work to do with her before I would be willing to risk that much again. Most people, when they get pregnant, don't feel that they're putting themselves at risk; but once you've had a premature baby, you know that there is a lot of risk involved.

DR. BRAZELTON   There sure is. It takes so much out of you to raise a child like this successfully, as you're doing with Adrienne. But it can make you feel drained and empty and wonder if you've got anything left for another baby.

FRANCI   It does. Adrienne is so incredibly important to me, that I wonder . . .

DR. BRAZELTON   You've got one love affair that's all-consuming; how can you have another one?

As we talked about another baby, Adrienne seemed to be listening to us. She even moved a bit closer. For the first time, she

A Sense of Self

wanted to include me in her play. I was beginning to feel that closeness to her that her parents spoke of. She was winning, when she wanted to be. As she became less wary, all of her body became more supple, softer. She seemed to relax and let me in to her world. I felt very drawn to this appealing child.

DR. BRAZELTON   You've done a wonderful job. It's exciting how far she has come. She's so independent.

FRANCI   It feels exciting to see Adrienne move out on her own, but I do have some qualms about losing her, losing our closeness.

A conflict every parent knows.

THE ISSUES

The task of encouraging independence and a sense of self in small children while also setting up firm and consistent limits is a complex one for any parent. For the parents of prematures, it is especially difficult. How did Franci and Mark manage to give Adrienne the sense of competence, of being able to manage for herself, that she is now showing?

A child with a sense of himself is brightly alive, sure of himself. He tackles a new problem with eager self-confidence. There are many ways that parents can encourage this, especially with a "vulnerable child."

They have to respect his need for autonomy and give him the chance to try things out – even to fail – on his own. They have to let him fall down, cry, and then pick himself up. Then they can reassure him that he's OK and that they are right there, caring. But they have to hold themselves back from rushing to pick him up, reassuring him too soon – before he's had time to realize that he's managed for himself. They have to let him learn to get to sleep without hovering. At first, when he wakens at night, they can "help him back down," or they can check "to be sure he's still breathing." Then they have to begin to let him get himself back down to sleep. They have to let him learn to feed himself bits of food without choking on them. They have to let him try out foods and refuse them, and tease them about what he'd eat and what he wouldn't. During this time most parents have a lurking fear that the baby won't get what he needs. Parents also have to learn to set limits, and to punish, even when they are not sure he deserves it, for sure limits are reinforcing to a toddler's sense of security. And, most important of all, they have to learn to detach themselves from the child's struggles in order to let them be his.

The tendency to create a "vulnerable child syndrome" around a premature baby, or around one with any kind of weakness or illness, is universal. Such a syndrome first involves the parent's perception of the child as threatened by everything, easily over-whelmed, and likely to die. The parent tends to hover, to protect the baby – rushing to him at every opportunity. At night, parents interfere with his sleep pattern. At mealtime, they feed him almost forcibly, and ignore any signal he may give of a need to feed or choose for himself. Under such circumstances, every area of the baby's developing autonomy or independence is likely to be in-vaded by well-meaning, devoted parents. Because of what they've been through, their goal is survival, rather than fostering the kind of independence in the child that makes for a confident, free person. Without meaning to, they deprive a child of the chance to try out his own developing skills, to make his own choices and mistakes, all of which foster a sense of excitement, of independence, and of self-confidence. A "vulnerable child" soon expects to fail, to be helpless, and he develops failure patterns, helpless behaviors which demand a parent's constant attendance. Feeding and sleeping prob-lems are almost inevitable. Punishment and limits in the second year seem almost impossible for parents of high-risk babies, and without a lot of effort such a child can become a "spoiled," unat-tractive toddler who does not necessarily value himself.

As soon as parents push a child to do things on his own, his competence will speed up. He becomes more energetic and self-

A Sense of Self

confident. The light in his eyes, the bright, self-assured look in his face, will grow daily. As a toddler develops his own sense of autonomy, he develops his own patterns for handling stress – withdrawing into a corner for a "time-out," sucking his thumb, twirling his hair, holding a blanket or "lovey" as he looks off dreamily – to reorganize his nervous system and to be ready for more.

There are classic ways to handle autonomy struggles. They usually happen at certain times: going to sleep, taking a bath, eating. Parents must work out ways for the child to communicate his needs, but also to fit into the family. For instance, if the child throws food, he can leave the table, but he cannot come back to the table. Both consistency and flexibility are vital, which means that parents must agree on a few important rules, and know when to allow choice in other areas. For example, a child doesn't want to take a bath. A parent might say, "Johnny, it's time for your bath, which toy do you want to take?" The child cannot alter the fact that he's going to take a bath, but he can decide what to take in with him. Or, at the table, letting a child eat by himself even if he gets food all over the table tends to minimize the struggles about eating. Again, choices are important:

"Do you want spaghetti or hot dogs?"

"Hot dogs." (You give him hot dogs.)

He says, "I don't want hot dogs."

You say, "Fine, you're getting hot dogs."

"I don't want to eat."

"Don't eat."

At that point, if he doesn't eat, let him down but do not offer food until the next meal.

These are just a few brief examples of the ways parents can detach themselves from the struggle to allow a toddler's independence and sense of autonomy to blossom. In my book *Toddlers and Parents*, many different families and children of various temperaments are seen working out these struggles. Franci and Mark, as parents of a once-fragile premature girl, have a particularly delicate balance to strike, but every parent must learn to step back as a two-year-old's sense of self is born.

The Sheehan-Weber Family

COMMON QUESTIONS

QUESTION   My daughter is a year old but was born two
              months early. She clings to me all the time.
              My older boy just made his own way. How
              can I get her to try things? What about prais-
              ing her a lot?

DR. BRAZELTON For her sake, watch for ways to let her do
              things herself, even if it takes twice as much
              patience. Then, after she's sensed her own
              achievement, you can reinforce her by letting
              her know how well she's done. That way her
              sense of having done it herself is its own re-
              ward. Your praise is secondary. You have to
              watch for this at every developmental step.

QUESTION   What about a child with a learning disability?

DR. BRAZELTON The most serious danger facing a learning dis-
              abled child is: the child's own expectation to
              fail. If this is not counteracted, by three and
              four years, he may give up and develop a pat-
              tern of failure which is more serious than his
              disability. Either he won't try, or he'll make a
              fool of himself, or he'll get himself in trouble
              – all ways of covering up this expectation to
              fail. We've seen it as early as eight months in
              babies with very minor brain damage. So, a
              parent's job is not to worry or to push, but to
              watch and gently support such a child as he
              very gradually learns each step. Then he will
              gain confidence as he does.

A Sense of Self

QUESTION   My two-year-old was premature and now is very disruptive in her play group. How do you achieve a balance between autonomy and discipline?

DR. BRAZELTON   Discipline is a form of security. A high-risk baby who has been through a lot may need the sense that he's strong enough to be disciplined. Without any limits, a child develops anxiety wondering how and when to stop herself. It's much easier for her if you say, "That's enough. You can learn when to stop. Meanwhile, I'm here to show you." It's harder to do for a child who was premature because you're so glad to see all that spunky behavior, but the child feels safer if you are firm.

QUESTION   Is getting through the night part of being independent?

DR. BRAZELTON   Absolutely. A child needs to develop his own ways of getting back down to sleep. Learning to sleep is an autonomy issue, and a child can be as proud of his independence at night as he is during the day.

QUESTION   How long is it OK for a child to be dependent on a "lovey"?

DR. BRAZELTON   A "lovey" is a very good answer at night. Many children use them to get back down to sleep. A "lovey" can be critical to a child's struggle for independence. She can fall back on it when she's in trouble. A "lovey" can be especially helpful in developing a high-risk baby's independence. Some children need them for the first six or seven years, so help your baby find something you can tolerate for that long. After

The Sheehan-Weber Family

you've taught her to be dependent, it is cruel to take it away from her before she's ready to give it up.

QUESTION My son just turned two and he's extremely independent around the house, but once we step outside he wants me to carry him.

DR. BRAZELTON He may need you for transitions like facing the outside world. I'd carry him for a minute and say, "You seem to need me for a little while until you're ready to walk outside yourself." That lets him understand his own pattern of dependency. He may also be teasing you a bit and acting out a kind of dependence he no longer needs. You could point that out to him, too.

QUESTION My daughter is very active and independent. Do you think there is such a thing as being too independent?

DR. BRAZELTON No. Not really. Unless a child pays no attention to discipline. Then, maybe you need to reevaluate your approach. In general, though, it's great to see the excitement a child feels about her growing independence.

QUESTION Aren't most parent-child struggles a question of autonomy?

DR. BRAZELTON Certainly. The testing that a toddler or a small child does involves parents' feelings about being able to control, and his need to rebel against control. Both sides care deeply, and in the struggle they learn to set boundaries for each other.

A Sense of Self

QUESTION

My children are pretty independent, except the youngest who is two. She's afraid to go out and explore. Do you think a day-care situation might help?

DR. BRAZELTON

I would suggest forming a play group with two or three other children her speed. They will learn from each other and develop greater independence. She probably has played a role of "baby" all along, which you've encouraged without realizing it. As a result, she may fall back on that role instead of learning to compete with her sisters. Learning how to handle her peers would give her self-confidence.

The Sheehan-Weber Family

Early Learning

❧

OFFICE VISIT

In my office, Mark and Franci offered Adrienne some crayons.

MARK　　　　　　　　Watch me draw your picture. Can you do this?

Adrienne watched quietly.

DR. BRAZELTON You are the best girl! Look, can you draw daddy?

Imitation is an important signpost of mental development.
For some reason, Adrienne is slow to respond today. Franci and Mark's anxiety comes right to the surface.

MARK　　　　　　　　I often wonder how much she understands.

DR. BRAZELTON All parents wonder whether their child's mental development is normal or not.

FRANCI　　　　　　　I certainly do.

DR. BRAZELTON Well, it's almost impossible not to, with a premature particularly. This is more than a game.

I wanted to observe Adrienne's reactions and also reassure her parents.

DR. BRAZELTON *I cover my eyes and play peek-a-boo. To Adrienne.* Now you do it. That's right, where's Adrienne? That's great. *Then I take apart a puzzle and ask her to do it.* I'm going to take them all apart; now you do it. You're trying. That's the way. *She does it in exact imitation of me.* That was smart. My goodness, that's wonderful. Let me show you something else. *I wind up a toy to make it run.* There we are. Now, let's do it again. *She tries to make it run, then she tries to wind it – showing another concept of causality.* She is doing fine. Now, for a trick. *I hide a toy under one, then a second, handkerchief.* No, no, not there. There it is! *She pulled up the second handkerchief.* That was so good! *To her parents.* What she has just shown is what we call the concept of "object permanence." Those three little tests, for a sense of imitation, causality, and object permanence, are windows into her brain and tell me whether it is functioning normally or not, which it is. When she was playing that game, and finally saw what I was trying to get her to do – her face lit up, as if to say, "Oh, this is fun!" Do you think she understands all the things you say to her?

FRANCI   She seems to. One day, I was trying to keep her occupied and I said, "Will you go in your room and get me a diaper and bring it back to me?" I was just trying to keep her busy, but she actually did what I told her to do.

DR. BRAZELTON   Isn't that interesting. She can follow through on a complex request.

MARK   But sometimes when I play with her she just sits there. She can be very stubborn.

DR. BRAZELTON   This is a time of negativism and independence. She may not want to let you know whether she understands. Not only does negativism

The Sheehan-Weber Family

come in but she needs time to take in what you're saying. Her hypersensitivity is still there. She's overcoming it all the time, and very successfully; but it means that it takes her longer to take in a command and respond to it.

As soon as I'd demonstrated her cognitive abilities, Franci and Mark questioned me about her language – was she behind?

DR. BRAZELTON Adrienne is only twenty-four months, minus three and a half months of prematurity, minus two months of illness. To expect her to function as a two-year-old might be a mistake.

Since they were worried, I asked them to watch for other signs of communication, for what we call "receptive language." Franci had answered this when she told us about Adrienne's going to fetch her diaper on command.

THE ISSUES

Parents today seem to be anxiously concerned with early learning. With a baby who has a slow start, parents' anxiety to prove she's OK may lead them to push her to do things before she's ready. Children should be allowed to pace themselves and to find their own way to achieving a new skill. An environment full of pressure is likely to become a strained, joyless one. Since we really don't know which parts develop at which age, it is critical to follow the child's own sequence and pace of development. When a child is "ready" to learn and achieve a new step, she needs little help doing it. But when she must learn it via parental pressure, she is going to have to spend energies that she will have to take away from other, perhaps more important, areas of her total development. This leads to children who, though precocious intellectually, are drained emotionally. Eventually they have trouble coping with the demands of our complicated society.

Early Learning

When there is a good relationship between parents and baby, and no impairment of the senses, speech and language develop naturally. When a mother looks at her baby, they make eye contact and the baby follows her face. When a father makes a noise, the baby responds accordingly. They must wait to give the baby a chance to respond. Interest on the part of the parents and good sensory capacities on the part of the baby are all that is needed for language to develop. If a baby does not have someone responsive to interact with, language development will of course be altered and delayed.

Practice and primitive imitation teach a baby the turn-taking necessary for language. At two months, she starts talking back with repetitive vocal sounds. At five months, a baby doesn't talk as much, but takes in what's going on and learns the difference between sounds. She begins to learn the meaning of the sounds made by her parents.

Up to nine to twelve months, the most important task for the parents is to understand what the baby needs. Babies begin to say "dadada," but without meaning. Somewhere between seven and fourteen months a baby begins to make her needs known by generalized means – grunting, pointing, gestures. This is nonverbal language. At around nine to twelve months babies begin forming words: "baba," "dada," consonant syllables. A little later they start associating sounds with phenomena, that is, "bow wow" for dogs.

At fourteen months a baby is able to understand commands like "no" or "put it in the basket." She begins to develop a sense of intellectual and verbal competence.

At around two, a child understands most everything you say to her and can follow a complete command. Most are able, quite distinctly, to put two words or double sounds together, with subjects and verbs. These are the precursors of sentences.

COMMON QUESTIONS

QUESTION Are there different kinds of learning? And how can I encourage them?

The Sheehan-Weber Family

DR. BRAZELTON   There certainly are different types of learning. First of all, there are four lines of development – motor, social, cognitive, and language. When one of these is taking a spurt (for example, when a year-old baby is learning to walk), other lines of development are likely to come to a standstill. It's as if there were an economy to learning processes in small children. The drive to acquire learning in all of these areas is very powerful. Unless something organic interferes, or unless the child has a poor early experience with learning, progress is spurred by the child's own inner excitement. Part of this eagerness to learn comes from identification with the parents. Then, as a child develops the exciting concepts of (1) objects and people as permanent, (2) cause and effect, and (3) imitation, everything speeds up. The best way you can foster learning in normal children is to reinforce their own excitement. If you put pressure on them to acquire skills that are beyond their own level, you might slow down one or the other of these lines of development without meaning to. Teaching them too much and too early in one area may stifle another. Follow your children's lead.

QUESTION   When you are introducing a new concept, how can you create a balance between motivating your child and letting him just follow his own interests?

DR. BRAZELTON   Learn to watch the child's reaction. When parents in my practice have pushed children to learn things "for Mummy or Daddy" the child may well do it – but the fire is not there. Later, this early experience may not generalize to learning more complex things. If the excitement of learning isn't there, a child who has appeared to be precocious may begin to fall behind her peers.

QUESTION   My daughter is sixteen months old. She was eating well, but now she's back to spilling things. She wants to experiment, and see what happens. Should I let her?

DR. BRAZELTON   It sounds as if she's using this experimentation to learn about food. She may also be testing limits to see how far she can go. If it doesn't matter, I'd let her alone. There's so much testing of limits in this second year. We used to feed one of ours in the bathtub so she could experiment all she wanted to.

QUESTION   Is there a good age to send a child to preschool?

DR. BRAZELTON   By age three or four a child needs social contact with peers. Preschool can enhance a child's learning to be in a group. Three or four is a good, but not necessary, time.

QUESTION   What about the difference between what children learn in preschool and what children learn who didn't go to preschool?

DR. BRAZELTON   A child's motivation for learning is more important than how early they learn. I wouldn't worry about whether you can provide preschool or not.

QUESTION   Do language skills reflect intelligence?

DR. BRAZELTON   Language skills do reflect intelligence, but they are only one reflection of intelligence. There

The Sheehan-Weber Family

are other signs, such as concepts of cause and effect, or imitating complicated tasks, which indicate whether a baby is intelligent or not. Language can be delayed for many reasons, including hearing impairment, which should be checked.

QUESTION   When should I start to worry about a child who is not talking?

DR. BRAZELTON   If a child is not babbling or making social sounds by five to six months, I'd worry about hearing. If a child is not saying any words by a year, or appearing to understand language by eighteen months, I'd have him checked. Most children start putting words together by two years. If a child understands you, I wouldn't worry too much. But if you *are* worried, get him checked out. There are many ways to do that, even in infancy.

QUESTION   We are going back to Mexico to live. Should I talk to my baby in English so she'll learn it?

DR. BRAZELTON   A parent should speak to the child in the language that comes most easily, otherwise the true emotional aspect of what is spoken is lost. She will learn your language and also the one that everyone around her uses.

QUESTION   My in-laws speak Chinese to my son all day long and we speak English at home. I wonder if the transition back and forth hinders him and pulls him back in some way?

DR. BRAZELTON   No. I think it's an asset to have two languages in early childhood. The daily exposure to two languages does not hurt a child's development at all and may help him sort things out in both languages. He may be slow to use each one fully, but he will be learning how to do that even before he speaks. Later, he'll be easily bilingual. All good linguistic experts learned early.

QUESTION I notice you change your voice and intonation talking to a child. Why is that?

DR. BRAZELTON I pitch my voice higher, because newborns and small babies are more responsive to higher-pitched voices. Also, when you change your voice to speak to a baby, she knows it's for her. Most adults talk right over a baby's head, so she learns that regular speech is meant for her parents. Baby talk is for her.

QUESTION My two-and-a-half-year-old son loves to recite the alphabet and count. I'd like to encourage this, but I don't want to push him.

DR. BRAZELTON Children are likely to push themselves, especially if the family is pressured "intellectually." Children will pick up this pressure. But social skills are very important at this age and are just as critical as language. So, I'd see that he learns other skills as well.

QUESTION If a baby starts talking early, will she learn to read and write early, too. Will it help her eventually?

DR. BRAZELTON Not necessarily. They are entirely different skills, although they are interrelated. It will depend on many things – especially on her motivation.

The Sheehan-Weber Family

QUESTION   My son is four years old and started stuttering all of a sudden. He rushes at speech and can't get it out. How can I help him? I know that if I push him it's liable to make it worse.

DR. BRAZELTON   That's right. Most children this age stutter and it's not anything to worry about. He is just trying to get all his ideas out in a hurry and his mouth can't keep up with them. It will pass in a few months – *if* people don't try to help him. Children go through periods of stuttering and stammering, just as they do through other things – like lying, stealing. All of these are normal. If you leave them alone, they will pass and your son will be as relieved as you are.

QUESTION   What are the early warning signs of dyslexia? When should a parent take these signs seriously?

DR. BRAZELTON   First of all, there is a tendency for these disabilities to run in families. Many of my patients in Cambridge who have learning difficulties in the early school years have fathers at M.I.T. and Harvard who had the same problems. They learned to overcome them. Maybe you could say they've even overcompensated. Most children are not identified until they hit school, when it is found that they have a hard time learning to organize numbers or to read words. By that time, they start to have an expectation to fail. This can be worse than the learning disability. For most children it's simply a matter of structure and time, but feelings of failure, if they are allowed to sink in, can last for life. We would like to be able to identify such children much earlier, to offer them

Early Learning

ways to learn which were appropriate to them, and to reinforce their sense of themselves.

QUESTION   What can a parent do to help?

DR. BRAZELTON   Children with learning problems often need more time to organize their thinking. Try giving this, especially in any new kind of learning situation. Also, you might help your child understand this herself. Say to her: "You need more time. Just take it easy and you'll get it. I used to be like that myself. Don't worry." That way, she knows you understand and she can also identify with you as she tries and worries. When she does go to school, be sure they test her so you can understand her ways of learning. We can tell a lot from tests these days and can help kids before they get into a pattern of failure.

The Sheehan-Weber Family Revisited

ﾑﾑ

I visited the Sheehan-Webers two years later in their two-family house in a Boston suburb. Adrienne met me at the door. She is no longer a preemie! She is a lovely four-year-old with curly blond hair, large blue eyes, and a charming grin, which spreads slowly from one ear to the other. Her features are very much like her mother's. The change made me gasp. She seemed so grown up as she held out her hand to me. I remembered her as a two-year-old, struggling for independence. Now, she is competent and secure. She remembered me and brought me presents, in the form of bits of wadded-up paper, obviously treasures.

As her parents and I started to talk, the illusion of a poised, older child began to disappear. She began to tease her parents to play with her, to pay attention to her – as I would expect of any four-year-old. At one point, having lost the battle to gain her parents' attention, she whispered in her mother's ear. Franci blushed and tried to put her off. Pretty soon, it became obvious that Adrienne wanted her bottle. Franci apologized to me for letting her still "be such a baby." I assured her that I thought it pretty appropriate for Adrienne to want a crutch to fall back on. The fact that she needed to regress, to fall back on a "bottle," didn't surprise me at all. She'd made such strides, growing up so much in these two years, that she needed ways to fall back and catch up with herself.

Her speech is that of a preschooler. She made up stories to please me. As a gift, she drew a picture of a multi-colored rainbow. It developed arms. I commented on how it was beginning to look like a person. She said, "No, it's a rainbow!" as if I were invading her territory. Franci quickly filled me in. Adrienne called herself a "rainbow girl." At that, Adrienne said, "I forgot her eyes." I said, "So it is a little girl – but she has no head. Can you draw it on?" Adrienne looked at me very seriously, to say firmly, "No eyes, no head!" That ended my invasion of her private space.

Her mother's attention had been drawn to this stubbornness, and she quickly added that she treated Adrienne as an "only child." Discipline was hard for Franci. "Limit-setting when you are working all day is so hard. I just want to enjoy her. I feel too guilty to reprimand her when I get home." I could see that Adrienne not only was used to a lot of their attention, but she knew how to get more. She is still very stubborn, I suspect. However, when they ignored her, or expected her to be on her own while we talked, she was cooperative. I did not feel that she dominated them or their lives in any serious way. The whole family seemed at ease with one another. No longer is Adrienne overprotected by her parents.

Adrienne is well within normal limits for her height and weight now. Her mother had worried about her growth earlier, but she is confident. Adrienne is tall like both her parents, and slender like her mother. Franci admitted that she still worried about how much Adrienne ate, but when we reviewed her meals, it appeared that she ate heartily enough. She showed no sign of deprivation. She just didn't want to eat when they wanted her to. She ate no breakfast, and explained to me, "I'm just not hungry then. But I eat later." Her speech is full of adult inflections and concepts, but they come out in childlike intonations. Just as she'd presented herself as quite grown-up when I arrived, and then regressed to a more appropriate babyishness, so did her speech regress as I listened. I thought this mixture was due to her being an only child – a very treasured one, who had learned to live up to the adults around her for brief periods but who still felt like a child and acted like one when under pressure.

Both parents are very busy. Franci works full-time as Nursing Director of the Ob-Gyn Ambulatory Unit at Beth Israel Hospital. This is a demanding administrative role, but, as she says, it gives her the freedom to stay at home with Adrienne when she has to. Mark works full-time as a psychiatric social worker; he is also getting his doctorate at Smith College School of Social Work, 100 miles away.

Franci still thinks of having another child. She wants to be with Adrienne more and is planning to work only part-time next year. Adrienne is taken to school by one parent or the other each day, and is very good about it. But one day after a vacation she said, "I'm not going back to school. My school days are done." This shook them. Mark took her back the next day, because Franci felt it to be too difficult to face Adrienne's resistance. On the way to school, Adrienne said: "I need to be grumpy. I'll be better later." When she got to school, all of her friends rushed to meet her, and the crisis was over. Later, when asked by her mother about school, she said, "It wasn't as yucky as I thought it would be." Franci realized then that it was more her problem about leaving Adrienne than vice versa. Adrienne's only real problem is that she won't take a nap at school. "But," Franci admitted, "she won't nap at home either. She doesn't like to sleep or eat – maybe it's just because we want her to."

Adrienne is a fascinating reflection of all of her parents' dreams – both grown-up and childlike. She seems to want to please them, and I felt her concern as they spoke to me about their anxiety over having another baby. Her eyes darkened, her face sobered, as they talked. She handed her mother a toy, as if to comfort her. I commented on her awareness of their concern and admired her desire to protect them. I thought that her resistance on the way to school, her grumpiness, would pass. They looked at each other as if to say, "She is growing up." It seemed painful to them to see the end of her childhood years.

"We'd like another baby, but I can't seem to get pregnant." Franci had had one pregnancy since Adrienne, which resulted in a spontaneous abortion very early. Since then – now fourteen months – she'd not been able to get pregnant, and they are concerned. Their doctor says that perhaps Franci is too tense, that if she'd relax she might get pregnant, but it's a vicious circle. No pregnancy leads to tension, and tension leads to no pregnancy. Her doctor suggested putting her on a drug to help her conceive, but this seemed to her another mark of inadequacy. She and Mark are determined to make it work. They laugh about it, "We are so concerned about *getting* pregnant, that we forget how awful it will be when we do get pregnant." Franci will have to be in bed for most of her pregnancy because of the incompetent cervix which

The Sheehan-Weber Family Revisited

resulted in Adrienne's prematurity. If she should get pregnant, she would have to quit her job, and he might have to postpone his Ph.D. It was like sitting on a bombshell.

When I asked whether their worries were about Adrienne, they had to smile. "No, at this point all our worries about her are low-level. She's doing so well now that we can't find anything to worry about. After the first horrible two years, the early months in the hospital, the repeated ear infections – she's never been sick since. It was as if she rounded a corner for us. Our fears about adjusting to her seem over. But it has shifted back to us. As soon as we knew she was OK, we began to want another."

They thought back to the stress that having a baby like Adrienne had caused them. In fact, it had started with Franci's first pregnancy, the first lost baby, the tubal pregnancy that ruptured suddenly and could have been fatal. This was followed by the miscarriage at twenty weeks, and the fear of loss was implanted. Franci began to feel at that time that it was her fault. She was feeling depressed, even then, and each subsequent blow reinforced these feelings. Adrienne's birth saved them and added a whole new dimension to their lives. At least, they say, they have a child! They can't imagine life without her. And it's this feeling of magic about her that seems to drive them on to want another. They never mention any fear they might have of losing her, but it must be there.

The stress on their marriage came to a head after Adrienne was two-and-a-half and they knew she was OK. "It was as if we dared now to reconsider our own relationship." The competition for Adrienne, first present in the premature nursery, built up throughout her infancy. At times, Mark felt shut out by Franci, that Adrienne belonged to Franci, not to him. Franci felt that Mark was detached from her and her suffering. They seemed unable to talk to each other. She withdrew; he became more optimistic, but as a defense. They missed each other.

They tried to communicate, but they found that each of them had set up a defensive facade. They realized that the succession of losses was too much for them, but they felt powerless to get back together.

The Sheehan-Weber Family

Finally, they saw a family therapist, who worked to help them communicate again. He encouraged them to unload their fears, their depression, and their defenses with each other. He spoke of the family as a canoe in which, when one stood up to yell, the other clung to the sides for fear it would topple. "No one communicated, and we were out of synchrony." As soon as he said they could both yell together, they began to be more open with each other. "I began to see how deeply Mark cared and wanted to protect me," said Franci. "She'd nearly died with the tubal pregnancy, and I felt responsible," said Mark.

By this time, as we talked, Franci and Mark had unconsciously moved closer together and were holding hands. Their concern for each other and for their marriage was being acted out for me. I commented that it seemed that this succession of traumas had brought them closer together. They had first attempted to handle the miscarriages and Adrienne's trying first two years by meeting the stress as two separate individuals. Each had done it separately, and successfully. Having a very sick, premature baby is a crisis for any family's equilibrium. Each member needs to establish his or her own integrity after such a perceived failure – such an insult. Then, after they recovered individually, they needed to relieve the pressure on their marriage. The cost had been great. As they said, "We hadn't been married long enough to feel like a team, to feel as if we had a base to fall back on. You have to know each other pretty well to dare to tell the other one how he or she is hurting you. We distanced ourselves, out of self-protection at the time, but then it was even more difficult to get back together. We didn't dare think about ourselves until we knew Adrienne was safe."

I was amazed at the honesty of this couple. They had dared to confront these tensions and to seek outside help. With the insights they gained from family therapy, they now seemed inseparable. As they said, "We don't need to prove ourselves any more. We need to keep working together." I felt the strength of this new level of adjustment for Mark and Franci. Adrienne positively glowed as she heard this last sentence. She certainly senses their anxiety – now focused away from her and onto a subsequent pregnancy. The mixture of precocity and childishness in her speech and her behavior was clearer to me now. She wanted to be babied, but she also needed to nurture her parents from time to time to prove that she was OK, that she was growing up.

Franci commented on this, too. "She is a very sensitive and caring child. When her grandmother was here and became ill, Adrienne went out of the room to get a quilt. She came back to tuck her grandma in with it. We were all so touched."

Mark and Franci have every reason to be proud. Their tiny, fragile, premature infant has indeed become their "rainbow girl."

The Schwartz
Family

❧

CHAPTER V

The Schwartz Family

The Schwartz Family

Family History

Kathy Schwartz is a nurse. She is a dynamic strawberry blond who carries everyone around her on a crest of happy excitement. Joel, her husband, is a physician, an eminent specialist in cancer. Although he must work with depressing situations, he too conveys confidence and enthusiasm. Dark, curly haired, he smiles a great deal, demonstrating his deep interest in everyone around him by his eager listening and participation. Joel is very involved with his children, Kevin, aged six, and a little girl, Jaime, aged three. Like many fathers today, he does half the caregiving and half the housework. Although the Schwartzes are well off with two salaries, they all participate in the chores. Family life together is their greatest pleasure.

Kathy comes from a large midwestern family. She is the second oldest of four children, with brothers on both sides who adored her. When a younger brother was born, Kathy was expected to care for him. Probably this nurturing experience led to her future career in nursing. She says that as far back as she can remember she has always wanted to take care of people. Joel was born in a suburb of New York to a middle-class family. One of two boys, he was from an early age expected to become a doctor, and he hardly remembers when he didn't share this expectation. He was a resident at the Beth Israel Hospital in Boston when he met "the beautiful new nurse on the floor." She was in training when they courted and wed. They lived near the hospital for the first few years. Kathy taught Lamaze childbirth classes, and after Kevin was born she became affiliated with a group of obstetricians. She has been a member of their team ever since. As each child was born, she took off from work long enough to get the baby started, but after six months she felt obliged to return to work. They have always had a live-in sitter, an older woman who cared for the children while both parents worked.

The Schwartz Family

After training in cancer treatment at the National Cancer Institute, Joel was offered the position of Director of Oncology at a teaching hospital affiliated with the University of Massachusetts Medical School in Worcester, fifty miles west of Boston. Because of this, and because of their desire to raise their children with a sense of safety and community, they moved to Grafton, a suburb of Worcester. There, in a lovely eighteenth-century house, they settled their family and sitter. Each drives to work separately in the morning – for Kathy it is an hour of commuting each way. But both Kathy and Joel feel that the move was a good one. Kevin and Jaime have been healthy and happy in Grafton. They are bused to a private school nearby where each is doing well. With both parents working, these children had become close and relied deeply on each other.

Now Kathy was expecting a new baby. The balance that this busy family had so far managed to maintain was about to be shaken.

A New Member of the Family

ॐ

OFFICE VISIT

When the Schwartzes came to my office, before the birth of the baby, their main concern seemed to be the adjustment of the two older children. Although these children were old enough so that most parents would not have been concerned, Kathy and Joel were aware that a new member of the family could disrupt the balance they'd achieved with Kevin and Jaime.

Kevin was a serious little boy who wore horn-rimmed glasses. He looked like an intellectual already. He listened intently to everything we said, although he tried to appear nonchalant. Jaime is a lively little girl who teases her parents mercilessly. As they tried to talk to me, she found endless ways of inserting herself into our conversation. She was obviously used to a great deal of attention. Now that the focus of the family was shifting to the new baby, she tried to keep the spotlight.

KATHY   This is his favorite position. *She pointed to her baby's feet which showed through her abdomen, as they kicked.*

DR. BRAZELTON Look at him go! How has it been for you over the past two months?

KATHY   Um, long.

DR. BRAZELTON Long? *The other children came up. Jaime stood in front of her mother so I couldn't talk to her.* How are you? My name is Dr. Brazelton. What's yours?

The Schwartz Family

KEVIN   Kevin. *Looking me over, up and down, very se-*
                   riously – no smile.

DR. BRAZELTON   Hi, Kevin. How are you? *To Jaime.* What is
                   your name? *No answer. She doesn't even acknowl-*
                   edge me. What's her name, Kevin?

KEVIN   Jaime.

DR. BRAZELTON   Jaime Schwartz, I'm glad to know you. Come
                   on in and play; there are lots of toys over there.
                   You can go over and play with them. I'm really
                   glad you're all here before the baby comes, so
                   I can get to know you as a family. Maybe I
                   can help with whatever adjustments are nec-
                   essary when the new baby comes. What sort
                   of questions have you got for me?

KATHY   Kevin and Jaime seem to be more worried
                   than we'd expected. Especially at night.

DR. BRAZELTON   What do you mean?

Kathy showed a certain anxiety with her rapid hand movement. Her eyes were serious as she watched the children.

KATHY   Well, they're getting up a couple of times dur-
                   ing the night, Jaime particularly. They seem to
                   need to have spot checks to see if I'm still
                   there. One day I found all the new baby's
                   clothes in the trash. Neither would admit it.

As we laughed over their pointed mischief, the children melted
away – into the toy corner. The laughter barely camouflaged
Kathy's concern. Kathy knows her older kids need her, especially
now, but so does someone else. That is her conflict. Joel brought
out an ultrasound photograph of the baby. The children came over.
How awesome, scary, this must be to a three-year-old.

A New Member of the Family

KEVIN   *To Jaime.* Can you find Max's nose? *He and Jaime have named the baby Max.* There. Very good. Eyes. No. Yeah. Nope, up, up, up. Right there.

There was a greasy spot on the photo.

KATHY   Someone was trying to feed Max peanut butter and jelly sandwiches. It looks like you got it dead center into his mouth.

JOEL   Do you think Max is going to be a boy or a girl?

KEVIN   I'm sure I won't get my wish. I feel bad about my wish now.

JOEL   What's that?

KEVIN   I don't want to take care of two sisters.

JOEL   Oh, was that your wish? That's not so bad.

KEVIN   I know it's not.

KATHY   Kevin told me he's going to keep the baby in his room, and that I shouldn't worry if the baby cries too much because he can take care of it.

JOEL   Are you worried that the baby is going to cry a lot?

KEVIN   Yes, that's what I was just going to say. You ripped it out of my mouth.

The Schwartz Family

Kevin has been through all this before with his sister Jaime. His apprehensions are from his memories; now they are becoming immediate again.

KEVIN   I have a feeling that he's going to wake me up, you know, in the morning.

JOEL   With his crying?

KATHY   Well, how about if we let Max sleep in his own room, and then you can come in and help when you want to.

KEVIN   But when is he going to come out?

KATHY   Pretty soon, I think.

JOEL   *To Jaime.* How do you feel about Max coming into the family?

JAIME   I like him, I love him.

KATHY   Kids, feel right here! What do you think he's doing in there?

JAIME   Kicking.

KATHY   He sure is kicking.

JAIME   He's very good.

KATHY   I wanted to ask about Jaime's stomachaches. Yesterday, all day and the day before, she's complained of a sore stomach.

DR. BRAZELTON Little girls this age often have them because they're beginning to identify with their mothers. They know women have bellyaches, but they don't know why. When they have a pregnant mother, of course, they identify with the pregnancy. Becoming like you is one way of hanging on to you when you go away and leave them or turn to the new baby. It's a normal way of trying to adjust. *To the kids who were listening seriously.* Do you know what? I want to get to know you both. Not just your mommy or daddy or even old Max. I hope you'll come play here some more.

KEVIN   *To Jaime.* Do you want to play baby?

JAIME   OK. You be the baby. *They go over to the doll corner.*

"You be the baby" meant that she wanted to mother Kevin, but in their game, Kevin plays the father's role. Jaime picks up the doll and targets a kiss, then a punch, right at the baby's belly. There's already rivalry between them for the baby. Jaime pouts when Kevin plays father to the doll. One really fascinating thing about watching these children play is how interdependent they are, how much they depend on each other. I noticed that when Kevin started playing daddy with the baby, she withdrew. A second child feels deserted when the older child turns to the new baby. That's going to be hardest for Jaime.

KATHY   When Jaime was born I felt guilty spending time with her because Kevin's needs were so great. He expressed them openly, verbally and physically. What I tended to do was leave Jaime in the bassinet all the time. I would feel guilty when I was trying to nurture her. Now I worry that I'm leaving her again.

How heavy guilt can be for a mother. Jaime was indeed afraid of loss, but it wasn't just Kathy. It was Kevin.

The Schwartz Family

DR. BRAZELTON   One thing that helps your feelings as much as it helps the children, is to have a special time for each one of them. You can talk about it all day. It's not that you have to have a lot of time for them, but you have to have some time when each one becomes very special, with nobody else around.

KATHY   Yes, I should do that more.

DR. BRAZELTON   There's no magic remedy to cure a child's resentment of a new sibling. But it's a help that Kevin and Jaime have each other. Not only does Kevin work on his problems through her, he gives her a chance to play the mother figure and take care of him. The other side of it is that being this close is going to be hard for Jaime when the new baby comes because Kevin will turn to the new baby. Your leaving her may not be as big a threat as Kevin's leaving her.

Kathy seemed surprised and maybe relieved at this thought.

IN THE DELIVERY ROOM

One month later, Kathy went into labor, attended by Dr. Robert Margulis. In the labor room, everything went well. Kathy was experienced and relaxed about her labor. She worked hard. Joel supported her, rubbing her back, encouraging her to pant and push. Dr. Margulis stayed with her throughout this perfectly natural birth – no medication, no anesthesia, no forceps, no episiotomy – a fairy tale delivery that most people hope for but many never experience. Both parents were jubilant at the last push – and here was "Max"!

A New Member of the Family

KATHY   He's a redhead!

JOEL   Like you!

Jeremy Daniel Schwartz (the name his parents had chosen) was robust, ten pounds, four ounces. Kathy held him on her abdomen – skin to skin.

KATHY   Hi, sweet guy.

Then, the natural anxiety:

KATHY   Why isn't he crying?

JOEL   He's fine.

KATHY   Max, hello, my love.

JOEL   There you go! He's not Max. He's Jeremy!

KATHY   He's here.

JOEL   Well, he sure is a Max.

KATHY   He's a gigantic guy. You want to open your
                   eyes? How come he has this rim? This rim
                   about his scalp? *Kathy was looking for things to
                   worry about.*

DR. MARGULIS   That's pressure on his scalp from the pelvic
                   floor.

Jeremy's feet were twisted in the position in which they'd been in, up around him in the uterus; they would need attention.

KATHY   Could you put up my johnny? Just pull it up,
                   just cover him up. Oh, he feels so good next
                   to me.

The Schwartz Family

Meanwhile, Dr. Margulis had asked Joel to cut the cord. Soon afterwards, I came to check Jeremy, having been asked by the parents to do the initial assessment. I used this testing, as I often do, to help Kathy and Joel know their baby better.

DR. BRAZELTON   Watch while I test his hearing. *I talk to him.* Hey, boy, come on over here, fellow. Come on. Come on, come on. Don't fuss at me. Come on, big boy. *That's* the way! Oh, you're so strong to handle – such a tight little package. *He turns to me. Then I ask Kathy to talk while I talk.*

KATHY   Come on, baby, come on. *He turns to his mother's voice.*

DR. BRAZELTON   He prefers his mother's voice to all others. *To Joel.* Now let's you and I talk.

JOEL   Come on, Max. Come on, come on, come on, come on. Absolutely! He knows me. *The very second Jeremy turned to his father's voice, out came his father's arms.*

While I checked Jeremy, his parents watched eagerly. Every infant comes with a repertoire of reflexes. Stand him up, and he'll automatically take his first step. Talk to him and he'll turn. Let him see your face and he'll follow it. Touch his face near his mouth and he'll try to suck on your finger. Jeremy, who had received no drugs through his mother's bloodstream during this unmedicated birth, was alert and responsive.

Kathy looked at Jeremy's turned-in feet, but didn't say anything. She spoke of his navel, as if avoiding the issue.

KATHY   Check that belly button to find out whether it's an innie or an outie.

A New Member of the Family

DR. BRAZELTON   His belly button is fine, but his feet have a positional deformity. Not too bad, though. They're turned from being up around him in the uterus. This inversion of his feet may need to be treated with casts eventually, but that will do the trick and he'll be perfectly normal. *I then asked Nancy Poland, a neonatal specialist, to perform the Brazelton Neonatal Assessment Scale on Jeremy. This is a test to tell whether a baby is neurologically normal, how alert he is, and something about what kind of baby he will be to live with, at first.*

MS. POLAND   He's got wonderful head control. Contrary to what a lot of people think, babies are really quite strong in their neck muscles. Look at him, he's doing his homework. *Jeremy followed her face and voice. He turned his head to look for a rattle. On his feet, he walked, controlling his whole body's musculature.*

When performed in front of parents, these tests show parents that their baby is not only normal but wonderfully capable. Kathy and Joel were particularly concerned with his feet, so his excellent attempts to use his walking reflex were reassuring to them.

MS. POLAND   This is a very good exercise for him. *As Jeremy walks and sits.* And you notice that his eyes are bright and awake.

Infants not only see at birth, but they can track a moving object.

MS. POLAND   Look at that, isn't that amazing? He's very interested. And look how relaxed you are, Jeremy, I can tell because your skin is nice and pink.

The Schwartz Family

Joel and Kathy could see that Jeremy was fine. After a few days' recuperation and discussion with the doctors of how to treat Jeremy's feet, the Schwartzes brought him home. Kathy found that breast-feeding went very smoothly with Jeremy. She stayed home from work for four months, as the family of five reorganized itself and Jaime and Kevin became acquainted with their brother.

THE ISSUES

PREPARING THE SIBLINGS. As we saw in the office visit, Kevin and Jaime were getting ready for the new baby. Because their mother is a childbirth educator, this may have occurred sooner than in some families. Formal preparations for the new baby needn't come till the last few months, when the pregnancy has more reality. If the subject is brought up too soon, months seem interminable to a child. What siblings need preparation for as much as the baby is the departure of the mother to have the baby. This is the culmination of the long period of pregnancy and the inevitable pulling away from the older children that occurs. Any pregnant woman unconsciously withdraws into herself. It's critical to give children a reason for that kind of withdrawal and for your eventual departure. Jaime would be even more frightened if Kathy hadn't talked about it with her.

BONDING. In her work with new parents, Nancy Poland is very sensitive to the bonding process. She encourages husband and wife to hold the baby, and shows them how the baby responds to light and sound. For many mothers, the first contact is the delicious feeling of the naked baby on their abdomens, the moment after birth. Many doctors and midwives follow the same procedure Dr. Margulis follows, that is, putting the baby against the mother's skin right away, and not cutting the cord until it stops pulsating. Dr. Margulis often asks the father to cut the cord. He points out that this can be a moment of strong emotion, the moment of separation for mother and baby.

A New Member of the Family

"The nice thing about a birthing room," says Kathy, "is that you're not moved around, and that you can stay together." Most hospitals give the mother her baby to hold in the delivery room. She is allowed to inspect her new baby, and may be encouraged to nurse. All of this is done under a warming light, to protect the baby from its tendency to lose body heat. The mother has the chance to prove to herself that the baby is intact. When she can touch and nurse him, she will feel that he's hers and that she is already getting to know him. The longing for a baby in pregnancy has raised both her anxiety and her energy to "bond" to her. It certainly is an important and exciting moment. Fathers participate in this experience, and, of course, it is highly important to them, too.

In some cases, however, the importance this short period holds for the future of the parent-infant team has been overrated, and mothers (or fathers) who did not have a chance to "bond" may feel that they will never entirely make it with their baby. It is important to keep in mind that bonding is only an initial part of getting attached to a new baby. Bonding is like falling in love; it is only the first step. Attaching to the baby takes many months – months of hard work, diapers, crying, adjusting one's lifestyle. Getting attached and getting to know one's baby – and yourself as a nurturer – is a long-term job. For these reasons, I am fighting for legislative changes that will allow enough parental leave around a new baby's birth. Four months is a minimum amount of time for parents to attach to a new baby – emotionally and physically – and to relate to each other as a family. It takes months, not minutes, to be securely bonded to your baby, and confident of oneself as a caring parent.

PRIVACY. Because of the need for intimate time together, a family must guard its privacy through this early period. Every well-meaning visitor amounts to a disruption, a set of new stimuli to adjust to. The drain on already overtaxed systems is out of proportion to the value of a social visit. I recommend that parents set a rule that no one except immediate relatives (or real helpers) be allowed to visit in the first week or ten days at home. This gives new parents and older children a chance to get back to being a family. It gives the mother a chance to rest and recover from her physical exhaustion. The father can use his energy to become an active participant.

RECOVERY. Learning how to become a new, reorganized family takes a lot out of everyone. The more the parents care about doing well by the baby, the more demanding this period can be. Postpartum depression is universal and its causes are partly physical and partly psychological. On the physical side, there is the tremendous reorganization that a woman's body must go through after the delivery and the inordinate amount of energy she must expend to recover. The psychological adjustment makes a tremendous demand also. In our society, there is not much support, and the challenge of a new baby becomes even harder. There is a built-in loneliness which the mother is likely to experience, and an expectation of being on her own during this critical time, which adds to the pressures.

A normal part of postpartum depression and readjustment is the ominous feeling of something about to happen. The feeling is irrational, and yet it cannot be dismissed. The expectation of doing the perfect job of childrearing makes both new parents tense and uneasy: "Is this right? Am I doing the right thing?" It may help them realize that the baby is also in a state of transition. Mistakes at this time will be absorbed better than ever again. The disruption of labor, delivery, and the new world leaves the new baby out of balance. A parent's main job is to support the baby's readjustment, and to get to know her. There is no "right" way to do this and it takes time. Fortunately, most babies are not that fragile. New babies have tremendous capacities for adjusting to change and disruption. The mistakes parents make will bother the parents more than they will the baby.

At birth, a baby's sensory world enlarges rapidly and often overwhelms him. The inappropriate stimuli in newborn nurseries add to this barrage. Going home further disrupts the rhythms and any balance the baby may have achieved after delivery. This means that a disorganized, somewhat unpredictable baby arrives home that first day. There, he becomes surrounded by a protecting,

A New Member of the Family

nurturing atmosphere, but it will take him a few days to relax into it and to readjust. New parents can't be in a hurry.

Because babies don't sleep through the night, parents get little sleep, which adds to the exhaustion and tension. All babies cry, and many fuss more in the evening. As mentioned earlier, most babies seem to need a fussy period at the end of the day, to let off steam, for exercise, or for reasons we do not understand. It appears to be an almost inevitable part of their day.

Breast-feeding mothers have additional physiological demands on them. They should rest and drink an eight-ounce glass of something every hour that they are awake. In the beginning, it's better to follow the baby's rhythms and to feed on demand, if possible. After a week or so, when the rhythms fall into a pattern, it is time to try to establish a schedule that allows for the parents' needs as well as those of the baby. Waking the baby for feedings, every three to four hours in the daytime, will begin to set a rhythm. When the baby is ready, he'll stretch out at night.

Play periods, just after the baby is fed, are important for parents and baby. I recommend that parents set up at least two — one in the morning and one in the afternoon or evening.

THE FIRST DAYS HOME. A common danger of the first day home, when all the adults are tensely involved, is that they will overwhelm the new infant with too much fluttering attention. They may overstimulate at a time when he needs to readjust her regulatory mechanisms. It won't actually hurt the baby in any way, but it may prolong the period of readjustment.

Feelings of competition among the adults around a newborn – such as a spouse, nurse, grandparent – are normal. A wise mother will welcome the father's desire to show his affection and push him to do some of the ordinary but, at this point, exciting things for the infant. For example, he can help at bathtime, change diapers, or offer water in a bottle. The new father will have made it through the lying-in period on nerves, alternating between exhilaration and anxiety over his new responsibility. He is likely to feel shut out by his wife's readjustment and by his still-remote relationship to the new baby. This is the time to capture his interest in his child and to engage him as a real participant.

The Schwartz Family

COMMON QUESTIONS

QUESTION   What about paternity leaves? How important is it for a father to take time off work with a new baby?

DR. BRAZELTON   It's a vital opportunity. Any father who is able to take a period off from work, to be home with the baby, and help in the process of forming a new family will never regret it. A glimpse of the baby after work is not the same as participating in everyday care.

QUESTION   What should the role of the grandparents be?

DR. BRAZELTON   Any family who is lucky enough to have helpful, available grandparents nearby should surely use them. They can be a help to everyone – especially an emotional help. The difficulty these days is not only physical distance. New parents struggle so hard to establish their own independence that they tend to push grandparents away. Even if a grandparent says "Do it this way!" and you say, "I'd never do it that way!" they have helped you shape your own decisions. When parents feel cared for by their own parents, their confidence and enjoyment of the baby grows enormously.

QUESTION   When I go to nurse my new baby, my nineteen-month-old daughter is interested in nursing. What should I do?

DR. BRAZELTON   Let her watch you. Let her climb up to see what you are doing and, if she wants to, even let her try to nurse. She won't know how, but

A New Member of the Family

at least she won't feel rejected. She'll probably only try it once. There's a statistic that shows that women who have watched their own mothers nurse, even when they were very small children, are more successful at breast-feeding. Letting your daughter participate is ingraining an important experience for her future.

QUESTION   I'm breast-feeding on demand. Sometimes I feel like all I do is nurse the baby twenty-four hours a day, and I feel it's not fair to the rest of the family. .

DR. BRAZELTON   Are you jumping too soon just to keep the baby quiet? Demand feeding in the beginning is critical until you get to know the baby's rhythms; then it's time to balance his needs with everyone else's. Are you feeding him at times when he might be able to learn to do other things? Let him sit in a baby chair and look around. Let him get frustrated at times. Frustration can be a powerful force for learning, as long as it isn't overwhelming. Check to see if anything is wrong. Then let him fuss for ten or fifteen minutes. Offer him a mobile or something to watch. After fifteen minutes, then go to him to try out other things, or feed him, if they don't work. But it would be better for all the family if you could push him to be more self-reliant, to learn to wait three hours between feedings. After the first few weeks, most babies can do this.

QUESTION   What can a pregnant woman do to prevent postpartum depression?

DR. BRAZELTON   Nearly every woman goes through some physiological letdown or depression after the de-

The Schwartz Family

mands of pregnancy, labor, and delivery. Respect the need for rest and for being taken care of. Most new mothers weep easily, feel out of control. They are likely to feel alternately euphoric and lethargic; they may even feel crazy. Remember, it's universal and will pass. If the depression continues and doesn't get any better after you have recovered physically, get some help. It's not easy for the baby if a mother stays depressed. Plan ahead to get help from your husband and use him to be a monitor on how you are doing. Though you can't prevent these feelings, you can reduce the sources of stress that make them more severe. Recognizing that they are universal will keep you from adding a whole other layer of anxiety.

QUESTION

How do the pain-killing drugs mothers take affect the newborn?

DR. BRAZELTON

Almost all drugs cross the placenta to get into the baby's bloodstream. The fetus's liver and kidneys must then detoxify them. As long as the baby is connected to the mother, her liver and kidneys also work to cut down on the level of circulating medication. At the point where the cord is cut, the baby is left to deal with the medication alone. Her liver and kidneys are immature and don't get rid of any of them very easily. Hence they circulate longer. In addition, her brain is immature and more vulnerable to the effects of medication. We have found that a newborn baby's behavior can be depressed for as long as a week by large doses of barbiturates in labor and delivery. With small doses, given only once just before delivery, the effect is minimal and very transient. If you need a dose to relax the cervix right at the end, the longer you wait to get it the better it will be for the baby.

QUESTION   What do you think of Dr. Leboyer's ideas on birth "without violence"?

DR. BRAZELTON   The main value of Dr. Leboyer's technique was to enhance the childbirth experience for both mother and baby. At a time when women were not given choices about labor and delivery, his ideas were thrilling. Now conditions have improved except in a very few backward hospitals, and women are given the chance to be awake and participating. Another of his important ideas was respect for the baby's need for gentle handling at birth. One could hardly argue with this. However, a cry right after delivery isn't necessarily a bad thing. Crying gets the circulation going and oxygenates the lungs rapidly. It can be a real help in arousing a somewhat depressed baby.

QUESTION   Do the Leboyer techniques have any dangers?

DR. BRAZELTON   In some cases. For instance, lowering the lights in the delivery room makes it possible to miss cyanosis (a "blue" baby). It isn't necessary to have it that dim. Not cutting the cord for a long time may carry the danger of overloading the baby with more blood from the placenta than he needs. He may have to get rid of it later by blood breakdown and severe jaundice. Immersing the baby in water after delivery to extend the feeling of being in the uterus is romantic but the water must be adjusted to just the right temperature, or the baby can lose critical body heat in a very short time. Loss of body heat can put a newborn quickly into shock.

QUESTION   When can I take the baby outdoors? What about cold weather?

DR. BRAZELTON   Give the baby the first week to achieve a balance and to stay away from other people's infections. Then you can take her out in almost any kind of weather. Dress her as you would yourself. Watch her color to see whether she's too cold or too exposed. Her skin will turn blue or too pale if she's cold. She'll turn bright red if she's too hot.

QUESTION   When can I expect my infant to sleep through the night?

DR. BRAZELTON   Sleep is one of the biggest and most unpredictable issues with a new baby. They don't usually begin to stretch out at night until eight to ten weeks of age, although this can vary a great deal. By four to four-and-a-half months most babies should be sleeping for eight-hour stretches at night. I'd wake a baby every three to four hours to feed during the day. This will help him stretch out when you leave him alone at night.

QUESTION   Should a breast-feeding mother let her husband give the baby a bottle at night?

DR. BRAZELTON   A breast-feeding mother can let up once a day to allow her husband to feed the baby a formula. Wait until your milk is established and you know she won't turn against the breast.

A New Member of the Family

She may prefer the ease of getting milk from a bottle if you do it too often. If your husband does one night feeding, you can get a long stretch of sleep. It will help you physically and psychologically, and will give him a real feeling of closeness with his baby. One bottle won't interfere with your milk supply. More than that might. One warning: If the baby is working hard and efficiently to suck milk from the breast, she may be so efficient that she gulps down a whole bottle of milk like an elevator dropping down an elevator shaft. It may well come up just as fast. Her father will feel like it's his fault – when she spits up the feeding. Be sure to use a slow nipple, so that the feeding takes about fifteen minutes. Afterward, he can prop her head at a 30-degree angle for another fifteen-minute period before he bubbles her. In a semi-upright position, gravity will help to hold the milk down, and the bubble will still come to the top of her stomach. Many babies need to be propped before they are bubbled, especially if the feeding was noisy and quick.

QUESTION   Is it all right to use a pacifier?

DR. BRAZELTON   Sucking is very important to the baby's feelings of security and well-being. The choice between a pacifier and the thumb is up to the parents. I prefer the thumb because it's right there, and a fetus sucks on its thumb anyway in the uterus. The thumb is under the baby's control and becomes his way of calming down to get to sleep, comforting himself, or focusing his attention so he can take in his world. It's a way to regulate himself.

QUESTION   Is it common for mothers to feel that they have to wean their child when they go back to work?

DR. BRAZELTON   I hope not, for it isn't necessary at all. If a woman gets her milk established before she has to go back, then she can pump at work to keep her milk coming. If she breast-feeds at least three times a day, she'll keep her breasts stimulated enough. She can feed in the morning before she goes out, breast-feed when she returns from work, and then wake the baby for a third feeding before she goes to bed. That way, she'll keep her own milk coming. The baby can be fed with formula while she's gone. She will find herself looking forward to a cozy breast-feeding at the end of every day, a reunion with her baby.

QUESTION   What if nursing is painful?

DR. BRAZELTON   In the beginning this is often true. It surprises many women. The pain comes from the spasm of the milk ducts all through the breast as the baby starts to suck. Most women's breasts are comfortable after the initially painful first few minutes. After the early weeks, this initial pain starts to disappear. Experienced women encourage new mothers not to give up. Sooner or later, the pain will go.

QUESTION   How much is the baby affected by what the mother eats? Are there foods to avoid?

A New Member of the Family

DR. BRAZELTON Very few. Maybe chocolate, onions, or garlic, but I'm not even sure about them. However, you should avoid any food you yourself have been allergic to, for you might set off a similar allergy in your baby. People tend to blame mothers' diets whenever a baby fusses unpredictably. Most fussing in the newborn period is not due to food she's eating. To restrict a woman's diet because her baby fusses is absurd. Women should lead as normal a life as possible while they are breast-feeding. It should be a wonderful experience in every way.

QUESTION When are the best times to wean a breast-fed baby?

DR. BRAZELTON There are many developmental periods, spurts in development when babies are not as interested in sucking or breast-feeding. These are best times for a mother to wean her child. One such point occurs very commonly at four-and a-half to five months. The baby gets a burst of awareness of sights, sounds, people around her. She won't stay at the breast unless you feed her in a quiet, dark room away from everyone else. If you want to continue nursing, keep your milk coming by feeding her morning and evening, out of everyone's company. The rest of the day, let her be distracted. If you want to wean her, this is one possible time. Any developmental spurt – sitting at six, crawling at seven months, stranger anxiety at eight, walking at twelve or more months – is likely to be associated with a lack of interest in settling down to nurse. You can use those periods to wean her if you yourself feel ready.

The Schwartz Family

QUESTION   With all the pressure being placed on mothers to breast-feed nowadays, what about women who never breast-feed or can't?

DR. BRAZELTON   The most important goal of any feeding, as important as the nutrition, is a feeling of closeness and trust. You can do that with a bottle. But *never* prop it. Food is only half the feeding. The positive emotions and stimuli that are transmitted back and forth during a feeding are just as critical as the food itself.

QUESTION   How important is the newborn period to the baby's later development?

DR. BRAZELTON   It's the base on which your relationship is built. You get to know each other, build up expectancies for each other, and a sense of trust. Don't expect these months to be tranquil. Anxiety, turmoil, and euphoria are in the nature of this turbulent period. Out of this chaos will come order, close relationships, and a greater understanding of yourself and the baby.

Fears and Fantasies

OFFICE VISIT

When the Schwartzes brought Jeremy in for his six months' visit, Kevin and Jaime played in the corner with the dolls and dollhouse while I talked to the parents. Since Jeremy had just been nursed and was quiet, I could hear the conversation in the corner. Jaime had the mother doll and Kevin, the father. Both were hovering over the two baby dolls in the dollhouse.

KEVIN	. . . If you weren't such bad kids, we wouldn't have to leave you.
JAIME	Where are you going?
KEVIN	To have a baby, silly. Aren't you coming?
JAIME	I'm scared. Last night I had a bad dream.
KEVIN	What?
JAIME	I dreamt about a wicked witch. She came and took the baby.
KEVIN	Witches don't want babies. They only want older kids.
JAIME	But I'm scared, and the parents aren't here.
KEVIN	*Changing the subject.* Let's have the baby doll. Get it over there in the corner.

The Schwartz Family

JAIME	*Taking the baby doll and holding onto it.* You're my sweet baby. I love you, and I'm feeding you. *She puts the baby to her own breast.*
KEVIN	Here come the older kids. Watch out!
JAIME	Stay away from my baby, you kids. You might hurt him. He's mine, not yours.

Kevin hits the baby with one of the dolls; they both giggle excitedly.

JAIME	If you kids are going to hit my baby, you'll have to go to bed. I'm going to leave you and go to work! You're . . .

At this point, they realized that we were listening. They looked embarrassed and immediately shut up. Both were obviously trying to cope with the readjustment to the new baby. They were mixing up their reactions to the new baby and to their mother's return to work. Their reactions to the baby are universal ones: because they were "bad" or inadequate, their parents needed a new baby; if they did not hide negative feelings, there would be retaliation in the form of witches. Their play was so openly revealing that I felt they unconsciously wanted us to hear it. I hoped to be able to use this to interpret to Kathy the many and predictable concerns which the baby had brought to the surface for Jaime and Kevin.

KATHY	Jaime talks a lot about her witch dreams. Most nights she wakes up every three to four hours, with bad dreams.
DR. BRAZELTON	Everything Kevin does, she imitates precisely. Many of the things she may be saying to you about the monsters might be coming from Kevin.

Fears and Fantasies

KATHY   You know, when I asked why she talked about death, she said Kevin said we're all going to die, then she went on about the baby. The other day, there was an endless sea of puzzle pieces on the floor. I said, "This is endless," and Kevin said, "Everything has an end, even people." He bounces a lot off of her and leaves her with anxieties. She's the one who has nightmares, or comes in checking to see if we're still there.

DR. BRAZELTON   All children have fears and begin to have dreams about monsters when they are about three and four years. They get afraid of fire engines, about dogs barking, all sorts of things like that. These fears are normal and a healthy part of their adjustment. When they've settled the autonomy issues of the second year, they begin to feel aggressive and to want to take control. With these aggressive new feelings come anxieties: "If I'm this aggressive, what's going to happen to me, or what's going to happen to the people I'm aggressive toward?" At nighttime this comes to the surface, in the form of nightmares.

KATHY   When she gets up and talks about monsters, should I help her look under her bed? Sometimes we do a monster search at bedtime.

DR. BRAZELTON   Fantasy, monsters, all need to be taken seriously. Sure, join in with them. You might say, "I'll look under the bed so you won't have to worry about the monster, but you and I know that there are really not any monsters under there."

The Schwartz Family

KATHY — Should I explain their feelings about the baby, too?

DR. BRAZELTON — Sharing their anxiety is very important. Discussing it is equal to sharing it. Give them a chance to tell you about their worries and fears. Children also need to know that when their fantasies get out of hand, somebody can say, I'm in control. It's a kind of testing of the water.

Kevin and Jaime were listening.

DR. BRAZELTON — You know what, I'm going to help you and Kevin and your mommy and daddy learn to handle the new baby. I'm going to help you be sure things go all right. Your mommy says you have been worried about things in your dreams. I'm explaining that they're important dreams and worries. They help you get used to having a new sister or brother.

THE ISSUES

The function of our fear is to help us survive. Our earliest survival reflexes are those of startling and of crying out. They are adaptations to sudden change, inherited from our primate ancestors. In response to danger, our adrenalin goes up, and our heart rate and respiration increase. All this makes our brains better oxygenated so that we are more alert and ready to face the danger. This alarm response helps us adapt to crises all the way through life. Most developmental spurts are accompanied by some form of alarm reaction.

As we get older, and experience the behavior of others around us, we learn to fear. It is taught by parents and other people around us. This learned fear continues to create a physiological response.

Fears and Fantasies

First instinctually, and then more consciously, the baby senses how important the parents are for her survival. Fear of abandonment is usually experienced by a child for the first time as a conscious notion at about five months. When the mother or caretaker leaves the room, or goes out of the child's sight, in earlier months, the child could be content, but at four to five months, she starts to cry and to show distress because she doesn't understand that the parent is still there. The child has no cognitive way of integrating the images of the parent and knowing the parent will come back. So she feels abandoned. This fear of abandonment crops up again at developmental periods when independence is taking a spurt. For example, when she begins to crawl at eight months, when she can walk or toddle at twelve months, increasing fears of strangers and of abandonment concur. Fear accompanies the wish, the capacity to separate. Separation for a small child carries with it a heavy price: exhilarating but scary. A child in a new stage of development needs reassurance, a secure place with her parents.

With the awareness of independence in the second year comes a new set of fears. Among others there's the fear of flushing a stool down the toilet, or the fear of going down the drain with the water out of the tub. This is the child's concern about her body being intact. She doesn't understand what is not part of herself. A parent can give comfort by holding a child, being there, and flushing the toilet together.

One of the most popular displays at our Children's Museum in Boston is a huge toilet that children can climb into and then climb out the other end, to see where their urine and bowel movements really went. Children of three, four, and five are fascinated by the chance to work out this fantasy. They line up for blocks to get in and out of it.

Children may still be confused about their body's boundaries, but they do understand pain, and they are afraid of punishment. By three, children begin to get concerned about being injured or punished for their bad feelings. For example, when a younger sibling enters the scene, and the older child resents the younger one or her mother, she may fear retaliation. She fears that her bad wishes will come true, and that she will be punished for them by bodily harm. At this age, children don't understand yet that their bad feelings and wishes won't come true.

Jaime's monsters are a displacement of her jealous feelings. No amount of reassurance will get rid of her fear of retaliation for her "bad" thinking. A fascination with monsters is an attempt to overcome them. Jaime is trying to have her monsters become acceptable, as she is her bad feelings.

Fears can be caused by various kinds of stress, such as the hospitalization of a parent, or, of the child herself. Other situations which cause fears are the first day at school, or camp, a move, separation from parents because of a vacation, any kind of change in child care. These fears can be compounded by aggressive feelings. For example, when a child starts school, if she's mad at a younger sibling or her mother, she may fear that something bad will happen to that person while she is away and that she will be responsible.

When talking about a child's fears, you always have to ask: whose fears are they? They may have been initiated by the developmental stages that the child is going through, but the fact is that parents can get pulled into the child's struggle and add their own worries to the situation. Fears then get accelerated. Families often need help in understanding what these fears are all about.

Books, records, and even TV can help children at bedtime with fears. There is a wonderful story, *Baby Sister for Frances*, about a new sister and the struggles that ensued. Such books help make fears less terrifying for the child.

OTHER COMMON FEARS. Young children mirror what a parent feels about bugs. You can bring them up to be friends with bugs. Let them handle one.

Fear of losing parts of the body increases when children become aware of gender differences. When a little boy sees a little girl for the first time, he worries that he'll lose his penis if he's bad.

Masturbation can bring new fantasies and fears. Children experience pleasure in handling themselves. When they're chastised for it, they fear punishment the next time they feel pleasure from that kind of behavior. Even without the parental disapproval prevalent in our culture, they may feel as if it were wicked to experience this kind of pleasure.

Some children fear meeting other children, fear being with another child, or fear that they will lose control because they've spent a long time keeping themselves in control during the day.

School phobias are also common. A stressful evening at home might trigger a reluctance to go to school, but if this persists after the situation has cleared and the child is still unable to go to school, parents should look more deeply at what is fueling this anxiety. There are often underlying fears of something happening to one parent or the other.

If parents understand their own issues about these stages, then they can deal better with their children. Many parents feel embarrassed by the fears in their children, because they do not realize that fears are developmental and universal. When parents understand their own feelings and feel empathy toward their child, the fears will be less overwhelming to the child.

THE FANTASY WORLD OF THREE- AND FOUR-YEAR-OLDS. At about two-and-a-half a child learns about herself by play and fantasy. She can divide this new-found person, herself, into two parts; one part of herself can be a baby, wetting diapers, and the other part becomes a successful grown-up child, toilet-trained. Neither is yet entirely acceptable. Both are her. One part at a time can be played out in fantasy.

At this age, a child often finds she has acted upon her "bad" wishes, as well as dreamed about them. When she realizes her acts are real, or even if they're still just wishes, then she's caught. For though she knows the difference between these magical wishes and what is real, she pictures that those around her see her badness. It becomes a scary game – unless she finds a way out. Often she finds one: she can lie or blame the misdeed on a friend, an *imaginary friend*. These imaginary friends become important as ways of dealing with reality, of not being too overwhelmed by it.

Imaginary friends, which begin at about two-and-half to three, are especially important to a first or only child. The friends take many forms – a bad friend who perpetuates all of the misdeeds, and a good friend who takes the role of the ideal self. They are usually private, because when they get shared, they are subject to ridicule and they lose their magic. This magic is precious. The value of the imaginary friends in enriching a child's private world and in working out her real problems is obvious.

LYING directly about situations often becomes the next step in the testing of a child's world. When the imaginary friends cannot be held responsible for actual or wished misdeeds, she begins to assume responsibility but denies it at the same time. Lies protect this precious world, and it is a real surprise when they are taken too seriously by adults.

STEALING may also begin at this age. It is a common way for a child to try out some of her wishes. Lying and stealing are common in three- and four-year-olds. If parents take them too seriously, they are likely to project them into the child's future as problems. Overreaction can set them up as patterns. Parents can be reassured that lying and stealing are "normal" at this age.

The developmental sequence of fear, fantasies, imaginary friends, lying, and stealing is an inevitable one. When parents understand this, their own anxieties are lessened.

COMMON QUESTIONS

QUESTION   How do you help a child with a special fear, such as fear of the bathtub?

DR. BRAZELTON   Take her in with you, hold her tight and gradually lower her into the water. Over time, she will lose the fear. Don't force her, because there is no hurry.

QUESTION   Are these fears different at different ages?

Fears and Fantasies

DR. BRAZELTON   They certainly are different and you need to address them differently. A baby may be afraid of slipping or of being overwhelmed by older children near the water. Many children, even those who have even learned to swim in the first year in these swim programs, refuse to go near the water in the second year. A new awareness of water and its danger suddenly overwhelms them. This must be respected. Gradually, using you as a safe base, a child can work out his own sense of mastery.

Fears for a three-year-old are more complicated. They go with fantasies, with sensing aggressive feelings and with an unconscious fear of retaliation. A parent can defuse newly burgeoning aggressive feelings by giving a child permission to be more open and aggressive. But it is important to show that you will put limits on aggression. If these feelings are aimed at a new baby, assure the child that you will stop him when he needs it.

QUESTION   What about separation fears? What can a parent do to relieve them?

DR. BRAZELTON   Of course, it depends on the age of the child. The inevitable ages are: at eight months, a fear of strangers; at twelve months, a fear of strange situations and of being left; at one-and-a-half to three years, fears of separation. These can go on to build into more complicated fears. I would always warn a child when you are going to leave, let her know whom they will be with, and when you'll return. This builds up a sense of trust. If you sneak off, you may save yourself a crisis at the time, but you create an anxious child, wondering when the next desertion will occur — and the next,

The Schwartz Family

and the next. If you prepare children ahead, by introducing them to the substitute caregiver while you're there, you are passing on the mantle of responsibility to the sitter. A child can protest safely while you are there, but she is likely to accept the sitter after you're gone. When you return, remind her that you'd prepared her and now you're back. This gives the child boundaries for her fears.

QUESTION

How can a parent help a child who is scared of being in the hospital?

DR. BRAZELTON

Prepare the child ahead by describing everything and stay with the child as much as possible during the hospital stay. Most children's hospitals not only allow but encourage parents to stay with their children and to prepare them when they must leave them. I would even encourage parents to avoid a hospital that didn't allow it these days, or to try to change the policy through legal measures. We now know how much it will cost the child afterward. Children need their parents' presence in a crisis. At Children's Hospital in Boston we also have child activities people who are well trained in child development and who plan daily programs for each sick child. We are learning how to compensate these feelings of depression and to speed up a child's recovery.

QUESTION

When a child begins to fear that his bad wishes will come true, how can parents know this, and what can they do?

DR. BRAZELTON

This is part of a normal developmental process in the three- to six-year-old age group. If the child develops fears or a new kind of fearful-

Fears and Fantasies

ness, I would look below the surface. Is there a reason for this? Is he adjusting to a new baby or to a pregnancy? Has he had any traumatic experience that you know of? If specific events or reasons have triggered his fears, I'd address them openly. If not, maybe he needs more permission from you to be aggressive or to be more experimental. Maybe you have him under a tighter rein than you realize.

QUESTION   My three-year-old recently asked me why there were no flowers in the winter and we talked about how flowers die and grow back in the spring. Then she asked me, "Do people die?" How would you deal with that?

DR. BRAZELTON   Don't say that people grow back. She won't believe you. But use such an opportunity to discuss everyone's fear of death, of loss. We haven't many opportunities in the USA to discuss these feelings with our children. We should value the chance. For children need to hear that we are afraid of death and loss, but we've learned how to cope with those fears. They need to hear from us about any religious convictions we may have. These are opportunities to share those convictions. If such a question leaves us speechless, we pass on only our own fear.

QUESTION   What about fears caused by family stress? How does a parent work those out?

DR. BRAZELTON   The same way. Openly discuss the stresses — how and why they occur. Help your child understand that you are all under stress, and you are all working on this together. Fears are a normal, healthy response. If he's afraid of specific things, like a dog, accept it, but help him see that it's not the dog he's afraid of. Help him pat a dog if he wants to and hold onto him around dogs for a while. Assure him that all children are afraid of dogs at some time or other and it will pass.

QUESTION   My daughter has an imaginary friend, Lucy. How do I act when she talks about her. Do I acknowledge her existence? What do I say?

DR. BRAZELTON   Aren't these friends wonderful! I'd stay out of it except when you're invited in. Otherwise you might ruin her friend for her. When Lucy does something bad, accept it at face value, but say, "Well, you and I know Lucy shouldn't have done it. I think you're lucky to have such a friend to show you what you shouldn't do and to get you out of trouble. I love Lucy!" In other words, accept what she tells you, but gently let her know that you both recognize the falsehood. It's a marvelous stage of learning about what is right and what isn't, and to use a friend as a buffer is ingenious. A first child is lucky to have such imaginary friends. Second children are rarely allowed to play things out in fantasy. The older child is always there to correct her.

QUESTION   We were in an automobile accident and now my son plays at "car crashes." I think he is really affected by this accident.

DR. BRAZELTON   Of course he is. Playing it out over and over is a way of working out all the anxiety. When you can accept it and talk it out with him, you'll see his anxiety begin to evaporate.

Fears and Fantasies

QUESTION   Even though I know lying and stealing are common in preschoolers, how can I teach my child not to develop them into habits in later life?

DR. BRAZELTON   By not taking them too seriously. If you over-react, you create too much anxiety. This, then, is likely to confirm it as a habit. Accept the child's behavior on the surface, but let her know that you both recognize the reality. If it's happening repeatedly, I'd look for stresses on the child. When you find and understand them, I'd share that with the child. Every time you can accept and understand a struggle she's going through, you have the opportunity to help her understand herself. It can be a real breakthrough for her.

QUESTION   How do you differentiate between lying and pretending? My son makes up the most fabulous stories.

DR. BRAZELTON   I'd find ways to encourage your child's creativity and play fantasies. Pretending and lying about something are very different. Yet up to a certain age children actually believe their pretending is real. It is important to play it out with him so he can learn the difference over time.

QUESTION   My three-year-old has developed a fear of the dark and doesn't want to sleep alone. She is a pretty timid little soul, anyway, and we don't want to make her more anxious. How do you suggest dealing with that?

The Schwartz Family

DR. BRAZELTON There are ways in which a parent can deal with a child's fear of the dark: keeping a light on, giving her a "lovey" to sleep with. I'd help her to talk about what she's worried about underneath, if you can figure it out. Also, maybe now it's time to help her to become more aggressive and outgoing.

The Schwartz Family Revisited

On a chilly spring evening, my wife and I drove thirty miles out of town to see the Schwartzes. They live in a large white house with a tree-shaded yard.

After a pleasant social time, I began to question them about the three children who were asleep upstairs, and about their adjustment after the new baby had come. Their eyes sparkled as they talked. Their hands gestured with enthusiasm as they described their "now complete" family. Kathy said, "None of our fears about adjustment seems to have come true. Jeremy has been an easy baby from the first, and both older children adore him. You were absolutely right. Kevin, now eight, and Jaime, age five, seem to cling together to mother and father him. We feel excluded at times. They want to dominate him. They are an even closer team than ever before, and they sometimes overwhelm the baby with their good-natured but powerful parenting. Jaime and Kevin still sleep together in the same room. Thank goodness they don't want the baby in with them. When Kevin threatens to evict Jaime and take in the baby, she clings even harder to Kevin and won't let go. Kevin, of course, loves her attention. In fact, he needs her. Amazingly, she has taught him how to be outgoing. So he needs her, and he knows it. She, too, knows how much she needs him. She talks about 'my big brother' as if he hung the moon. Don't siblings have an enormous influence on each other? I don't know what these two would do without each other."

At the time, I wondered how much their strong interdependence had been determined by their parents' working. Kathy must have sensed my questions, for she said, "They have always looked after each other when we're gone. Now it's as if they were built-in caregivers for Jeremy. Kevin gets up to fix the others their breakfast. We give him an enormous amount of responsibility, and he seems to enjoy it." I asked whether he was identifying with his dad by being the breakfast-giver. Joel nodded and said, "I've always fed the children in the morning. Now Kevin and I do it together." I was reminded that in a two-parent working family, the whole family pitches in to make it work right. Kevin was already learning how to be a father in a working family. Wonderful!

Kathy and Joel began to talk about Jeremy's birth. Kathy remembered how easy the birth experience was: "By that time, Joel and I were very familiar with the birth process, labor and delivery, and with our ability to take care of an infant. Most importantly, we were confident in our ability to be parents to this new child." Kathy contrasted Kevin's birth with this: "Labor and delivery were absolutely frightening. Neither Joel nor I knew what to expect, even with our medical backgrounds. The thought of taking care of an infant was overwhelming to us. The thought of being a mother and father was completely foreign."

Kathy and Joel went on to talk about their "expectations" about parenting versus "the reality" of parenting. Joel stated: "With Kevin, we parented like we thought we *should* parent. We lacked confidence. We tended, therefore, to assume our traditional roles – I as financial provider and Kathy as the chief caretaker and homemaker."

This lack of confidence in parenting had had an effect on the way Kathy and Joel interacted with Kevin. Kathy noted: "Kevin was a quiet, predictable baby. He had a set schedule very early on in life. Because of this, I didn't feel as needed as I thought I would be. I was very uptight with Kevin, nursing him in a chair, for example, not feeling comfortable enough to relax in bed while I breast-fed." Joel agreed that all of their interactions with Kevin were less spontaneous and relaxed than those they experienced with their second and third children.

As Kevin grew older, he maintained his quietness and shyness. Kathy and Joel talked about how they had difficulty understanding this: "We didn't accept those qualities in Kevin." Said Kathy, "We tried to make him more like us, more extroverted and more social. His personality type was different from ours, but instead of respecting these qualities and learning from them, we magnified the differences. If Kevin had been a second or third child, when we already felt secure in our roles as parents, we definitely would have reacted differently. We would have felt less threatened by a personality different from ours and would have been more accepting of it.

"Kevin is still quite shy and serious and has a hard time with separation. He is extremely analytical. He has never accepted punishment without a good logical reason. In school, one of the kids pushed him and teased him because he wore glasses. I wanted Kevin to go fight back. He said, 'That may be the way you'd do it, Mom, but not me.' Instead, he asked this bully over to his birthday party and said: 'He wouldn't be a bully if he felt good about himself.' One of his teachers referred to him as Professor Freud because of the way he observes other children and his wonderful perceptions regarding them. This perceptiveness, of course, has carried over to the family. Once when Joel and I became too pushy with him, he said, 'We need a family meeting to learn to live together better.' Kevin still doesn't like large social gatherings, but, fortunately, Jaime has been able to lead him out of himself and to 'teach' him how to be more outgoing. Kevin has a number of really good close friends whom he chooses very carefully. He has a large number of interests and is extremely popular at school and in the neighborhood."

At approximately the age of two, Kevin was found to have a minor congenital problem. Kathy and Joel talked about how overwhelming this problem seemed to them as first-time parents who had definite expectations regarding their offspring. They talked about how they expected to have a first child with both a personality and physical make-up "perfectly matched" to theirs. When Jeremy was born, he too had a congenital problem, mildly "clubbed" feet. Kathy and Joel reflected on this: "When we saw Jeremy's feet, our hearts sank, and we wondered what else might be wrong with him. In spite of our medical training and my reassurance about such things to other mothers in my childbirth classes, when there was one problem, we were fearful that there would be more. Even now, when I view the film of the birth, I weep with emotion. I always focus on Jeremy's clubfeet first. Then I watch you examine him and help demonstrate his normal infant reflexes. I recall the tremendous sense of relief I felt that morning. I began to feel close to him and confident that I could mother him, and I have." Joel commented, "Our growth as parents helped us adjust more quickly to Jeremy's problem. Now we have adjusted to both Kevin and Jeremy's problems. During those early years when both Kevin and Jeremy needed to make frequent physician visits, we became aware that Jaime might feel left out, in that she was not making these 'special' visits to the doctor. This made us more sensitive to Jaime's needs during those times."

Kathy began to talk again about the "expectations" versus the "reality" of motherhood. "When Kevin was born, I thought that in order to be the best mother, I would have to be a 'full-time' mother, so I stopped working. But I found full-time mothering to be somewhat frustrating, exhausting, and, for me, not entirely personally fulfilling. I resented Joel's not needing to make a major lifestyle change, whereas I had. We became caught up in the traditional roles, thinking that mothering needed to be a full-time pursuit. I felt isolated with my feelings and frustrations and, living out in the suburbs, I felt more isolated still. Everything felt better after I returned to work. When Jaime was a baby, I knew I had to go back to work. Work for a woman can be very critical to her image of herself, and this was true for me. I still had some misgivings about leaving Kevin and Jaime to go back to work; however, after Jeremy was born, I felt much more self-confident, and I knew that I was a much better mother when I felt good about myself than when I didn't. We have been fortunate throughout this time to have excellent live-in help."

Joel then pointed out the very positive effect Kathy's going back to work had on his relationships with the children and his role in the family: "One of the consequences of Kathy's going back to work was that I broke out of my traditional father's role and became much more involved in the daily routines of the household – making meals, getting the children ready for bed, making their lunches for school and nursery school. I got to know them much better, and I enjoyed this more realistic, interactive role in the family." Joel and Kathy both felt that Kathy's returning to work had helped make the children more independent and flexible. Kathy commented on how "all the kids pitch in to make things go much more smoothly."

The Schwartz Family Revisited

If an on-looker sized up this dynamic family, he or she would see them as caring intensely about each other. Kathy and Joel had experienced the anguish and struggle which caring parents feel when they try to relate to a first child whom they find difficult to understand. Many parents feel the same kind of turmoil about one child in the family, most often their first child. In Kevin's case, it was compounded by a congenital problem. Kevin has learned how to cope with his parents and is learning how to cope with himself – largely through Jaime and now through Jeremy. He will be a wonderful father some day. Although his parents still worry about how to make life easier for this quiet, thoughtful, intellectual boy who has his own distinct style, all the time he had been teaching them to leave it to him. He is finding his own way, and has all the ingredients for success, even when it may not be their way. All of the fears and fantasies which he demonstrated, when Kathy and Joel brought him to me two years ago, have disappeared now – or gone underground. Did they serve a purpose in helping to prepare him for the new baby? He certainly has learned to cope with his aggressive feelings – not always by demonstrating an aggressive response, but by facing it with his characteristic intellectual solutions.

Each sibling has brought so much to the others. Kevin has dealt with Jeremy's intrusion into the family by almost smothering him with fatherly care. Jaime has already learned how to mother her brothers and also be Jeremy's "best friend." Kevin holds Jaime close to him – as a protection, as a way of entering a peer world, perhaps as a way of balancing his more introverted personality with hers. One wonders how they will face the separation in adolescence when it becomes necessary. Jeremy is learning how to lighten the seriousness of his intense family and to keep them all laughing. He is being mothered and fathered by four caring people – a lucky little boy.

Kathy and Joel have made their family work. Their investment in each other, in each other's work, and in their children's lives gives them the kind of fuel necessary to weather the normal stresses of living in a two-career family of five.

Learning to Be
a Family

❧

CHAPTER VI

એ**

Each of the five families in this book have had to face a number of normal "crises" which centered around developmental issues in their children. Each of the five felt "stuck." They could not resolve the problem, and they wanted to avoid being locked into a situation. Although these issues were not serious, they were costing the family its equanimity. In each case, the interview, and the opportunity to share their concerns in a "safe" place with someone who understood, was therapeutic for each family. They could uncover their anxieties, share with me their observations of their children, and work together toward a resolution. Resolutions take time to unfold, and, by revisiting each family a year or two later, I could discover how they had resolved their problems. In each case it was a matter of learning how to be a family.

Families are systems. Each is made up of members who are attached to, and who interact with, the others in the system. Ludwig von Bertalanffy (1968) was the first to point out that the stresses within a system can be used as powerful probes to test the strength of the system. Any system works to maintain a balance, which in turn supports each member within the system. In a family there are minor deviations, as well as temporary lags and spurts, in each person's development. However, within the safety of the enveloping family, self-exploration is possible, and each member can develop a sense of inner competence. When balance is disrupted, two outcomes are possible. If the stress is too great, or the system too weak, interrelationships break down, and balance cannot be restored. The family is no longer a viable system. If the family can meet the challenge, on the other hand, and handle the subsequent regression and friction that is bound to occur as the members reorganize, a new balance comes out of the disruption.

What is most important, as the family reorganizes, many more opportunities to learn how to cope with future stress crop up. Parents and children alike learn to recognize the regression that inevitably accompanies stress, as well as the sound of alarm which stress sets off. This alarm response triggers the mechanisms that we all have within us, including our anxiety, for adapting to stress. In this way, each so-called crisis – colic, tantrums, sibling rivalry – does more than speed up development of individual family members – it strengthens the whole system. These problems seem monumental at the time, and so test the adaptive capacity of each member. Each can learn about his or her relationship to the others. Once the stress is met and successfully managed, the family is reorganized, but on a different level.

Successful reorganization and the learning that takes place is rarely conscious within the family. In this book I try to bring the process to the surface so readers can see the kind of learning each family did as they confronted the "crises" that are so universally seen in normal child development. These stories should reassure anyone riding the roller coaster of parenthood.

For the individual child, no line of development – motor, cognitive, social, language – follows a continuously upward path. For each the course is jagged – a spurt, followed by a period of leveling off or consolidation; then a brief period of regression and disorganization in the child's development. This disorganization can surface in many disturbing ways – as a symptom like a nightmare or a stomachache or as a completely changed personality. This is frightening to parents, unless they see it as a sign of normal adjustment preceding new progress. These four developmental lines are intimately intertwined, and when one kind of development is in regression, it affects the others. It may appear that one particular line of development is deteriorating. The parents see it, and their concern or alarm guarantees that the whole family will be involved as the child regresses in preparation for a new developmental spurt.

Inevitably, when parents become aware of a developmental problem in their child, they regress back to the way they themselves dealt with it when they were children. All of us have "ghosts in our nurseries," as Selma Fraiberg (1959) pointed out. Each parent has unresolved crises from the past, which are called up when the child meets a similar challenge. As the child struggles, the parent is bound to be more deeply involved because of his or her own unresolved experience. This creates a kind of sympathetic turmoil in the parent which parallels and reinforces the child's struggles. Because of the parent's conflicting feelings, the likelihood that he or she will face the problem and be objectively supportive to the child is reduced. And the chance that both parent and child will become powerfully enmeshed in the issue is enhanced. In this way, what is really a temporary, usually minor, stage in the child's development can become a big family problem.

Each of us has these ghosts from the past, so it is no surprise that in raising a child parents often become enmeshed and so see the problem as bigger than it is. As long as these ghosts remain unconscious, they can dominate a parent's responses. But when they are brought out into the open, and the parent is made to realize why he or she overreacted, the effect is defused. A parent, then, has more choice in deciding how to handle a problem. We can never be rid of our ghosts, but we needn't be at their mercy.

Once parents begin to solve their part of the problem, the baby, or child, seems almost miraculously to know it. The child's behavior begins to change, to right itself, and development proceeds, as if the child knows that his parents are behind him once again. For instance, consider the gratitude seen in a toddler's face when the parent finally says "no" firmly, and stops him from the vicious circle of teasing and losing control. Family tension lessens, and the kind of relief felt by children when they see their parents back in control is reflected in many of the children in the five families. "Every baby knows" when he is, or isn't, creating a problem for the family.

By contrast, a baby who is in real psychological difficulty will continue to be stressed after a parent has acted. His face will look pinched and worried. His behavior will be irritating, and it will lead him into situations in which he can only fail. He will cry a great deal and his rhythms will be unpredictable. The clearest sign of such disturbance is the way the child's behavior affects others. Other children will shun him. Other members of the family will be affected and disturbed. Such a child should be seen as asking for help. A baby knows when he is in trouble. And if daily life with the child remains negative or stressed, if the parent feels overwhelmed by the situation, it is certainly time to get help.

Learning to Be a Family

Persistent behavioral deviations can be a reflection of a basic disturbance within the family.

In describing the five families, I've tried to show how, in a relationship with a listening, understanding professional, parents can dare to reveal their concern about their child's behavior and about how deeply it is affecting them. Together, they can peel away the layers of defense which have built up over the years. They can root out the ghosts from their own nurseries, which are echoed in the child's behavior and which turn it into a family problem. In such a relationship, the pediatrician or nurse does not hasten to assure families that their child's behavior is normal and that he or she "will outgrow it." Although such reassurance is accurate, it is premature. The professional who reassures parents rather than listens to what they are trying to say is missing an opportunity. At this moment of "crisis," parents are particularly ready to learn, both about the child and about themselves. When the parents' turmoil, or "alarm reaction," signals an unresolved conflict from the parents' own past, the listening professional can help them uncover it. A truly helpful and caring professional will create a relationship in which parents feel safe enough to allow themselves to see how their identification with their child has led to the family conflict.

Another important part of the pediatrician's role is to respect the parents' anxiety. Anxiety is "normal," valuable, and not a sign of weakness. By accepting the parents' concern, the caregiver conveys another message – that it *can* be dealt with. These unspoken messages make it "safe" for the parents to share their underlying concerns with the professional. As they deal with it, solve it, and learn from it, the whole family becomes stronger and more ready to cope with the inevitable series of stresses that will accompany childrearing in the years to follow.

Whenever I am able to participate with a family as it strives to uncover and cope with some of the issues we've seen in this book, I find my work deeply rewarding. I could never be satisfied treating physical disease and administering inoculations only. The child's and the family's development is a side of pediatrics and of preventive care that is too precious to neglect.

Across the country, the field of primary care for children is finally changing. It now includes much understanding of child development. With such training, pediatricians, nurse practitioners, and family physicians not only can participate in a family's development but also can prevent future illness and behavior problems in the child. But the change has been too slow. Most pediatricians still have not been exposed to the excitement of family dynamics that is involved in normal child development. Medical training, including pediatrics, is still heavily oriented to disease and physical development, and such dialogues as I have included here may not be appealing to some. The field of psychosocial development can be nebulous, and so may provoke anxiety in some health professionals.

I'm often asked by parents what I think they should do if their pediatrician is interested only in physical health and brushes aside discussion of behavior. "He'll grow out of it" or "Don't worry, it's normal" may be the extent of the advice. I urge parents to rely first on their pediatrician for support in what he or she can do well: following the child's physical development. They can then turn to other resources – child guidance clinics, child psychiatrists, psychologists, social workers – for help in understanding family issues *before* problems become deeply entrenched.

At Children's Hospital in Boston we have a multidisciplinary clinic for the inevitable, minor problems of normally developing children. We can, in an average of four visits, evaluate both the child and the family. We can help them address their own issues as separate from, but entwined with, the child's issues. We use this model clinic as a training opportunity for the Fellows who come to our Child Development Unit for postgraduate training. So far, fifty pediatricians, three nurse practitioners, and two child-development specialists have completed our fellowship. They are spread all around the country now, starting up their own research and teaching units within pediatric departments. There is a hunger in pediatrics for training in child development that is growing rapidly. The field is going to change.

Meanwhile, the hunger for professional support that I see in parents as they try to understand their children continues to grow, and at an even faster rate. I see this yearning as a force which will strengthen families and will enhance in them a sense of competence, as well as self-understanding in their children. While we in pediatrics struggle to meet this vital need of parents, I hope they in turn will recognize themselves, not only in the trials, but also in the splendid achievements of the five families who have so generously shared their lives with us.

Bibliography

Avery, M. E., and Litwack, G. *Born Early: The Story of a Premature Baby.* Boston: Little, Brown, 1983.

Bell, S. M., and Ainsworth, M. D. S. Infant crying and maternal responsiveness. *Child Development 43* (1972): 1171–1190.

Bertalanffy, L. von. *General Systems Theory.* New York: Braziller, 1968.

Bowlby, J. *Separation, Anxiety and Anger.* Attachment and Loss Series, Vol. II. New York: Basic Books, 1973.

Brazelton, T. B. *Infants and Mothers: Differences in Development.* New York: Delacorte Press, 1969.

Brazelton, T. B. *Neonatal Behavioral Assessment Scale.* London: Heinemann Medical Books, 1973.

Brazelton, T. B. *Toddlers and Parents: Declaration of Independence.* New York: Delacorte Press, 1974.

Brazelton, T. B. *On Becoming a Family: The Growth of Attachment.* New York: Delacorte Press, 1981.

Brazelton, T. B. *Working and Caring.* Reading, Mass.: Addison-Wesley, 1985.

Brazelton, T. B., and Yogman, M. W. (Eds.). *Affective Development in Infancy.* Norwood, N.J.: Ablex, 1986.

Dixon, S., and Stein, M. *Encounters with Children.* Chicago: Yearbook, 1987.

Field, T., Goldberg, S., Shuman H., and Sostek, A. *Infants Born at Risk.* Jamaica, N.Y.: SP Med Books, 1979.

Fraiberg, S. *The Magic Years*. New York: Charles Scribner's Sons, 1959.

Greenspan, S., and Greenspan, N. *First Feelings*. New York: Viking Press, 1986.

Klaus, M. H., and Klaus, P. H. *The Amazing Newborn*. Reading, Mass.: Addison-Wesley, 1985.

Lamb, M. *The Father's Role*. New York: John Wiley & Sons, 1987.

Lester, B. M., and Zeskind, P. S. A biobehavioral perspective on crying in early infancy. In H. Fitzgerald, B. M. Lester, and M. W. Yogman (Eds.), *Theory and Research in Behavioral Pediatrics* (Vol. I). New York: Plenum Press, 1982.

Patterson, G. R. Stress: A change agent for family process. In N. Garmezy and M. Rutter (Eds.), *Stress, Coping and Development in Children*. New York: McGraw-Hill, 1983.

Sammons, W., and Lewis, J. *Premature Babies: A Different Beginning*. St. Louis: C. V. Mosby, 1986.

Sander, L. W. The regulation of exchange in the infant-caregiver system and some aspects of the context-content relationship. In H. Fitzgerald, B. M. Lester, and M. W. Yogman (Eds.), *Theory and Research in Behavioral Pediatrics* (Vol. I). New York: Plenum Press, 1982.

Thomas, A., Chess, S., Birch, H. G., Hertzig, M. E., and Korn, S. *Behavioral Individuality in Early Childhood*. New York: New York University Press, 1983.

Turecki, S. *The Difficult Child*. New York: Bantam Books, 1985.

Yogman, M. W., and Brazelton, T. B. (Eds.). *In Support of Families*. Cambridge, Mass.: Harvard University Press, 1986.

Index

About the Author

Dr. Brazelton has been called the "pediatric guru of the 1980s." His insight into child development has not only influenced both parents and professionals all over the country, but also contributed to the lives of a whole generation of children. Professor of Pediatrics at Harvard Medical School, he is also chief of the Child Development Unit at Boston Children's Hospital and President of the Society for Research in Child Development. The Brazelton Neonatal Assessment Scale is in use throughout the world. Dr. Brazelton received the prestigious C. Anderson Aldrich Award for Outstanding Contributions to the Field of Child Development. Aside from his scholarly work, he is also known for his efforts on behalf of the four-month maternity (and paternity) leave and national support for families, through congressional appearances, lectures, and articles. In addition to his role as host for the cable television show on which this book is based, Dr. Brazelton is a contributing editor of *Family Circle* magazine and the author of seven treasured books for parents, including *Infants and Mothers, Working and Caring*, and *To Listen to a Child*.